BEFORE BLACKHAWK DOWN:

A Look Inside Pre-Civil War Somalia

Abdurahman Sharif Mahamud

PREFACE

In order to properly understand a country, you must not only look at its landscape, but also its people. When people today hear the word "Somalia" they often think of either pirates or "Black Hawk Down." It is true that the Civil War in Somalia has ravaged its landscape and its people. Many have fled the country out of fear of their lives and to make a better future for their families. Still, there is a longing for these people to be home. Somalia has a rich heritage and it is the hope of Somalis both home and abroad that it can be again.

This discussion of Somalia tries to shed light on a Somalia most people do not know. Many people see the Somalia today, stricken by a bloody Civil War. What was Somalia like before the Civil War? Who were its leaders? How were its borders formed? How did its people live? Therefore, this discussion traces Somalia's beginnings and brings us throughout its history and concludes just before the Civil War began.

If the people of Somalia are to end its Civil War and build a strong nation, they must remember where they came from. To shed further light on the history of Somalia, the second part of this book focuses on one man and how his life paralleled that of Somalia. He was both shaped by Somalia and he helped shape it. Sheikh Al-Sharif Mahamud was a prominent and respected leader in Somalia. He was born during some of Somalia's early turbulent years, saw and was a part of many of the countries struggles, and died just as the Civil War was taking root. Through this two part book, we can see how both a nation and a man can influence each other.

TABLE OF CONTENTS

PART I

PART II

Part I

A Historical and Analytical Survey of Somalia:
Early Beginnings to Civil War

Chapter I

An Introduction to Somalia

Somali is situated in the north-east corner of Africa and covers an area of 400,000 square miles in the region known as the 'Horn' of the continent. With a population of fewer than five million, the Somalis are basically a nomadic people and they cover the entire territory in search of water and pasture land for their flocks. They form their own groups or clan systems.

Previous to the penetration of the Europeans (British, French and Italians) in the mid to late 19th century into this region, the only outside influence came from the Arabs in the 8th and 9th centuries ~ho established Islam as the predominant religion. The Islamic religion became the basis of the Somali culture affecting both social and political views and leading to a unification of the Somalis, which is perhaps the one significant feature of the people of this region.

Beginning in the 1820s, the Somalis saw the initial attempts of the Europeans to establish territories in the Horn of Africa. From 1860 to 1897, the effect of partition on Somaliland by Britain, France, Italy and Ethiopia led to the creation of two self-contained and exclusive Somali territories: the British Somaliland Protectorate and Italian Somaliland.

Unlike other states and regions which became culturally divided by similar circumstances, this experience of alien rule increased traditional Somali consciousness of culture and national identity to such a degree that Somali nationalism became a politically motivating force in the transformation leading to the present Somali constitution.

This research will describe in as much detail as possible, the various forms of governmental administration through which Somalia has gone leading up to the effects which these numerous systems of administration have had on the present Somali government.

The uniqueness of Somali history lies, not in the trusteeship period of Italian rule beginning in the 1960s, nor in the period immediately following, but rather in the early, unhappy experiences, which resulted from dependence on European powers.

Because of its regionalism, the country is still a long way away from its goal of national unity, and because of the slow growth of its economy, it has not yet been able to achieve a high standard of social conditions.

Until the early 1800s, Somali, which occupies the northeast region of Africa, known as the 'Horn', had been relatively unexplored and therefore, unknown. In the 1820s, France realized the importance of establishing a port in northeast Africa that would facilitate trade in the Gulf of Aden. Their interest in the region aroused the curiosity of the British and the Italians who were, at that time, attempting to expand their territories.

The British found it advantageous to establish ports in the north and this resulted in the formation of British Somaliland. The Italians found that the Juba River, which emptied into the Indian Ocean, provided, but its many tributaries, natural and easy access into the inland regions and they settled into the southern area of Somaliland, which became known as Italian Somaliland.

It is natural, therefore, to assume that the penetration of these foreign entities into a politically and socially backward area, where the nomadic mode of life was simple and rules were self-imposed, would create serious consequences.
This was especially true, since the motive of these foreigners was concentrated on gain for their country and not on the wellbeing of the native Somalis.

Such was the trend until in 1960, British Somali land united with Italian Somalia to form the Somali Republic; it was an important step toward creation of a single Somali state, a new nation.

Outside the state or new nation separated politically and geographically were the areas of French Somaliland, Ethiopia, and Kenya who wished to join the Republic but without giving up considerable portions of their territory. Territorial claims, therefore, constituted the basic area of conflict preventing a united Somaliland.

It is important and noteworthy that these surrounding areas respected and admired the Somali, concept of a culturally defined national identity; an identity, which is part of their national heritage. However, in the background of every administrative change in Somaliland, has been, like a festering sore, the constant conflict over these borders.

Already much blood has been shed in efforts to achieve unification. I hope that unification may eventually be achieved through peaceful means. This study was undertaken not to write the political history of Somali land but to show how the numerous and rapid changes in government have led to the unique political situation in which the Somali Republic now finds itself as a nation. An important part of this study is to analyze how the various changes in the government of Somali affected the administration of its government.

Somaliland in East Africa has undergone numerous changes in its administration since the first century. The country covers 400,000 square miles and has a population of approximately five million people (Lewis, 16-22). Somalis are, by nature, a nomadic people. Because of this, and of their basic Islamic religious teachings, which determine their life style, the Somalis have found it extremely difficult to adjust to the many changes in government systems imposed on them over the years by foreign entities.

Influences Affecting Somalian Government

This discussion will deal with the administrative changes in the governmental systems in Somalia, beginning with the Italian Colonial days and continuing to the present. Because, as in any other area, the present system of government is direct result of events, which occurred previously, this study will briefly review these earlier systems for the purpose of demonstrating their effects. Among some of the earliest events in the history of Somalia which have a direct bearing on the current way of life are:

1. The introduction of Islam by the Arab ancestors of the Somali Clan Families, between the 8th and 10th century, which resulted in Islam becoming the area's dominant religion. Since

Islamic teachings are a way of life more than mere religious instruction, the Muslim population still adheres to the law of their religious teachings except when there is direct conflict with local laws, originating in pre-Islamic traditions, which are still strong outside the main towns. Although the Somali have no tradition of political unity, it is this heritage of cultural nationalism which, strengthened by Islam, lies behind Somali nationalism today and the fervor for a Greater [unified] Somali state (Lewis, 16)

2. Wars with Ethiopia, beginning in the fifteenth century and continuing today, arose for political, economic, and social reasons, and continue for the same reason. For Kenya and Ethiopia have little desire to relinquish very considerable portions of their territory, or to appear to encourage separatist movements amongst their already faction-prone populations. This conflict highlights the extent to which Somali nationalism differs from the nationalism of most other African states (Lewis, ix)

3. The period of treaty-signing in the late 1800's saw constant changes, beginning with the British treaties and followed by Italian treaties, and treaties between Ethiopia and France, Britain and Italy, regarding Somali areas. These treaties, dealing mostly with distribution of land, led to the United Nations stepping in and organizing Somalia under an Italian trusteeship in 1950.

4. The Italian Colonial era, beginning in 1893 and lasting through 1940, was initiated with the signing of an agreement between the Filonardi Company for Italy and Osman Mahmud and George McKenzie for the Imperial British East Africa Company (See Appendix I).

Organization of the Study

Chapter II offers as background, a brief history of the government systems in Somalia from before the Colonial era to the present. The periods included in this historical survey are as follows:

(1) Pre-Colonial (Clan-Tribal System),

(2) Italian Colonization (1893-1941; the Colonial Period
(3) The British Military Administration (1941-1950)
(4) The Italian Trust Administration (1950-1960)
(5) Independence: United Somali Republic (1960-1969), and
(6) The Somali Democratic Republic Scientific Socialist.

Chapters III through VI provide a general overview of different types of government from the Colonial era up to the present, in terms of administration and rule, concentrating on organizational structure, personnel systems and financial and economic development. The period covered by these chapters had the greatest effects on the present socio-economic and political conditions of Somalia today.

Highlights of Somalia's Government Development

During the pre-Colonial era, there was no governmental structure as we know it today; there was a clan-tribal system and because the Somalis were a nomadic people, this system was not regional-based, but rather traditional groupings of families with a common ancestor. The principle of government was that the people owed allegiance to their hereditary chief. Before the establishment of a centralized administration, the Somalis depended for the protection of their life and property upon their own group.

The Somalis believed that authority should not be vested in anyone person, hence the right of every man to speak at assemblies was an inviolable law. Tribal leaders were elected at these assemblies, major decisions concerning the groups were made by these leaders, and other matters were determined by a simple majority vote (Lewis, 212-228)

The period of Italian Colonialist system of government from 1893 to 1941, was notable only for the fact that Italian companies were constantly changing, each trying to defeat the other and all working towards their own profit and expansion of Italian territories. Among the ordinances drafted, one stipulated that:

"All uncultivated lands, unless their owners
were properly ascertained, were to become the

property of the Italian government. The
government was to have the exclusive privilege
of exploiting, or granting concessions to
exploit, minerals or deposits or any sort of
metals, minerals, mineral oils, and precious
stones. Special permission would be required
to cut wood from the forests along the lower
courses of the Juba and Webi Shebelle -
Somalia's sole source of wood .... Additional
clauses dealt with the regulation of justice
and commerce (Hess, 42)

Of significance importance during this period is the rule of the
Benadir Administration from 1896 to 1905, composed of the
governor, a group of local administrators on loan from the navy,
and a group of civil employees. This period was fraught with
discontent and in many cases, the administrative staff was itself
divided.

In substance, there was no financial administration, no
organization of justice, no military organization, no guarantee of
trade and communications, and no internal or external security.
This lack of organization resulted in below-level social
conditions for the Somali people.

When the Italian government assumed direct
administration, after years of avoiding its responsibility, it faced
the task of creating a colony and it evolved a system of
administration and a native policy which could readily be
extended into newly occupied territory.

Under the British Military Administration in the 1940s,
Britain tried to maintain a certain amount of unity for the
Somalis. It was a period of national consciousness as Fascist
social and political restrictions were removed. An Advisory
Council of traditional elders was formed but it had no governing
powers. Tribal agricultural and nomadic groups came together
with ideas for national unity, education, and constitutionalization.
Political associations were formed for "the wishes and welfare of
the inhabitants."

The Italians did not adjust well to these changes instituted
under British rule and with the help of the United

Nations, agreed on December 2, 1950, to a trusteeship under Italian administration on condition that they begin making plans with the Somalis for independence.

During this period of trusteeship, they increased education, trained civil servants, prepared democratic consultations, and in general, tried to win back the trust of the Somalis.

The first general elections to establish an independent government were held in 1956; all districts and provinces were placed under the direct charge or Somali administrative officers. The Legislative Assembly of Italian Somalia was granted full powers over the internal affairs of the country and despite much political dispute; Somalia's first prime minister took office on July 1, 1960, when the country became independent.

Administrative and bureaucratic structures had to be realigned and delicate political arrangements made. Great internal political unrest was evident during the first ten years of independence and very little or no progress was made as an independent state.

In October 1969, Somalia had a revolution which led to the forming of a Revolutionary Government. One year later, Scientific Socialism was declared as "the cherished goal of the Somali Democratic Republic" - a society based on labor and the principles of social justice.

The concluding chapters will deal respectively with recent developments leading to the present situation. Statistical Data will follow showing the overall growth of Somalia from 1960 to 1988.

Limitations Affecting the Study

This study has been limited by the fact that, until very recently, there has been no written Somali language; hence records are few, and for the most part, disjointed and incomplete. The method I employ is primarily that of historical descriptive analysis.

Most of the information from the Italian Trusteeship period was obtained from United Nations Visiting Missions' Reports and more recent developments were taken --

Development and Planning Projects issued by the State Planning *Commission* of *Somalia* and also from Recent Economic Developments and Current Prospects documented by the International Bank for Reconstruction and Development in Somalia

My own knowledge gained from personal experience as a native-born Somalian has been a primary source for this work. It is necessary to state that even though my own personal opinions cannot be documented, they are, nonetheless, based on fact. Maps, charts, and tables will follow relevant material and therefore will form part of the text. These documents will supplement the text and should facilitate reader understanding.

CHAPTER II

HISTORY OF GOVERNMENT SYSTEMS IN SOMALIA

The purpose of this chapter is to discuss briefly several stages through which Somali Government administration has evolved. This history begins with the early traditional clan system and covers the subsequent Islamic impact, especially in the 12th century; traces the effects of the British, Italian and French rule during the Colonial period; describes the nation's transition to independence in 1960; covers the coup d'etat in 1969 with its resultant new system of administration under Scientific Socialism; and finally touches on some more recent development.

Clan-Tribal System

The traditional Somalian society before the Europeans discovered the region in the late 1800s, has been described aS1democratic, almost to the point ~f anarchy, with every adult male having an equal voice in the Shir (the clan assembly). It has been said that every Somalian is a Sultan. Elders, not only old men, but also younger ones, who were seen as wise, acted as arbitrators, conciliators, and decision makers. The power of the Chiefs was personal, not institutionalized, and not dependent upon the charisma and leadership qualities of the individual.

The early Somalian society was essentially nomadic. Though there was no tradition of hierarchical government, during the sedentary agriculturalists, i.e., the non-nomadic segments, some elements of hierarchy did develop owing to the year-round attachment of people to one place and to the necessity of cooperative work on the farms.

In the traditional system, women of the sub-groups were excluded from participating in the Shir or clan assemblies. Arifa (traders in the farm market) might, however, participate in an advisory capacity in the deliberations of the Shiro Social differentiation within the adult male population was traditionally made on a secular or religious basis with every Somalian male being either a warrior or a religious follower.

Most traditional systems were based on subsistence agriculture or animal husbandry. Subsistence agriculture followed a traditional style which can only be described as primitive and with a low level of production.

The cash sector of the economy was non-existent. Illiteracy was high, urbanization was low; though birth rates were high, death rates were likewise high (Castagno, 147).

Legal System: The Dia-Paying Groups

Every Somali belonged to a dia-paying group. Dia is the compensation and is referred to as blood compensation. It was paid by a group when one of its members was found guilty of homicide. For lesser crimes such as insult or injury, payment was made in livestock. Sometimes, nubile women were used as payment by the offending group to the victim's group. Dia or blood compensation is illegal today.

Among the nomads, an inter-tribal unit or council determined payments of dia and the amount to be paid by offending groups. Among the agriculturalists, dia-paying groups were determined by village of residence or a group of villages, i.e., primarily by geography. Children automatically belonged to their parents' dia-paying group, and married women remained members of their father's group.

Among the nomads, both payment and receipt of compensation were group activities, not individual ones. A dia-paying group ranged in size from 200 to 300 males to 5,000. Among the sedentary farmers, such groups included whole villages and ranged in size from 5,000 to 10,000 men; they protected both the people and their livestock (Lewis, 212-228).

Structure of the Clan System

According to traditional groupings, there were six Somalian Clan-families. Each family traced its descent from a common ancestor from whom it took its collective name with the exception of Raha Weyn, which is a clan-family from a conglomeration of various clan sections. In many parts of Africa, the principle of government was that the people owed allegiance to their hereditary chiefs. In the Somalian pastoral society, this principle was replaced by binding ties of patrilineal kinship, which is the paternal line.

Somalis gave loyalty to their dia-paying groups, to their clans, sub-clans, and finally to their families. Before the establishment of a centralized administration, the Somalis depended for the protection of their life and property upon their own group.

A traditional clan system was characterized by an attachment to primordial values, a family-centered social structure, with limited participation in the world outside the tribe or village. The common struggle against, nature with inadequate equipment kept each family occupied with winning food and shelter and protection from enemies (Lewis, 216).

The traditional Somalian society was a bound Society motivated more by the desire to maintain what It had than by a desire to expand and improve its lot. Kinship was the primary basis for social integration and socio-economic standings.

According to I.M. Lewis,

> The Shir--clan assembly--was defined as
> an assembly for community. It exercised
> jurisdiction in all administrative, political,
> and judicial matters affecting the group, and
> consequently, enjoyed supreme prestige,
> status, and power among all its individual
> members. Loyalty to the Shir became an
> accepted absolute value (Lewis, 216).

The tribal system was the controlling force in Somalia from prehistoric times until the Islamic system, which began in the 9th and 10th century, but did not supplant the earlier system until the 12th century. Some remnants of the tribal system still influence Somalia.

The Islamic System

After the assassination of Caliph Uthman in Affan in Arabia in 656 A.D., Arab leaders failed to agree on the choice of a successor. As a result, the Muslims were divided into contending groups during the Caliphate of Ali Bin Abi Talib, with many wars arising among the groups.

Because of these events in Arabia, many "Sunni Muslims" came over and settled in Somaliland at the beginning of the 9th century (Somali and Arab League, 11). These Arab migrations to Somaliland and the building of settlements along its coastal region obviously led to the spread of Islam among the Somalis. By the eleventh century, most of the Somalis had become Muslims.

Government

It is uncertain when the Arabic title "Sultan" was introduced into Somalia. The government of the Islamic Sultan was usually hereditary and largely honorific. The Sultan of Adal, for example, who was the head of a Somalian clan, was not more powerful than any other Somalian clan elder, despite his high-sounding title (Area Handbook of Somalia, 64).

In some clans, the title passed to the eldest son and in others, to the deceased Sultan's brother. The Sultan of Adal developed a center of Islamic culture and Arabic trade in the ninth or tenth century with its capital at Zeila. During the 14th and 15th centuries, the Muslim Sultanate was engaged in a holy war with Abyssinia and in the 16th century, an Adal war broke out against Ethiopia. In Southern Somalia, however, the Sultanate was under total Arabic domination with Oman becoming the center of Arabic trade in Somalia (Somali and Arab League, 13).

The religion of Islam obviously then, had a tremendous impact on the cultural environment and the political administrative institutions of Somaliland, totally replacing the traditional Somalian structure of clan-government. The faith of Islam affected the values and behavior patterns of the entire Somalian society. Through the stability and durability of the

Shariah(Islamic Law) and religious thinking, this faith shaped the trends of Somalian institutions.

The Islamic Legal system, based on the Shariah or laws of Islam, was administered by a Kadis(jury) appointed by the Caliph which is the supreme religious authority. The Kadis were, in effect, legal secretaries in their respective provinces. Civil servants under Islamic rule were people who had studied the Koran. Political power and constitutional authority were in the hands of the Islamic clergy. Thus, administrative law and bureaucracy developed among the lines of the Koranic teachings; the religious and the secular were thus united (Lewis, 213).

Islam not only affected the administrative and legal institutions, but also, the political environment and culture of the people of Somalia. According to the Islamic law, God *is* the head of the community and the Muslims are his servants and are equals of one another. Islam, therefore, represents God's governing on earth.

The personal submission to the Shariah for the individual citizens implied at the same time, a social duty and precept of faith. Any person violating the Shariah is not only breaking a law but committing a sin. The Muslim community derives its existence and direction from the ethical and legal principles of Islam, the Koranic text and Mohammed's Arabic traditions (Fazlur Rahman, 212).

The Islamic society of modern Somalia is still deeply affected by these past events. Somalian Muslims have never stopped following the Islamic laws of politics and administration. Somalian Sheiks and men of religion occupy positions of great authority within the order of the administration.

In the past, the attempt was made to substitute the religious organization of the Brotherhood Movement for clan and tribal loyalties. In the way, the Muslim order contributed to national unity and sought to overcome sectional rivalries. However, given the circumstance of Somalian life and society, the only security was provided by small bands of kinsmen, so the loyalties of kin and clan remained paramount (Asad, 10). The Islamic religion has shaped the public and private life of the Somalian people. Somalis have always possessed their native culture, but Arabs and the Islamic religion contributed to their heritage.

On the whole, it can be said that Islamic law and administration, especially through its unification of Church and State, has greatly contributed to the shaping and improving of Somalian administration. Furthermore, its contribution has been felt through its delineation of a strong moral code, and by its ability to unite the Somalian people on a religious basis, a basis that superseded many clan and tribal loyalties (Bennett, 65 & 108).

The Colonial Period

Colonial history and African history go hand in hand as companion fields. The present Somali Republic, independent since 1960, is the political descendant, not of tribal Somalia, but of the Italian colony of Somalia as well as of its successor governments, the wartime British military administration and the post-war United Nations Trust Territory of Somalia under Italian administration (Hess, vii).

Because Somali land is so regionalized and because there were so many changes in government from 1884 to 1960 involving all the regions, trying to trace the history of these governments becomes confusing. However, an attempt; will be made to show these changes chronologically and by region and with the help of the following map, it should not prove to be too difficult.

The British ruled from 1884 until June 26, 1960 in the northern region of Somalia called the British Protectorate. In 1960, it united with the former Italian territory in the south to become the Somalian Republic.

In Southern Somaliland, two Italian companies, the Filonardi and the Benadir took over as administrators from 1893 to 1905. The Italian government, not satisfied with the administration, took complete control of the governmental system until 1940 when, because of an unsatisfactory Fascist regime, the British Military stepped in and assumed control of the administration. In 1950, the United Nations found it necessary to return the southern region to the Italians under a trusteeship agreement, which lasted until 1960 when Southern Somaliland joined with the northern British territory to form the Somalian Republic.

In 1859, the French in their exploration of the Red Sea, purchased the port on the Red Sea and by 1884, the French had occupied a small portion in the north of Somalia. The French did not relinquish their territory until June 27, 1977, and this small portion was included in independent Somalia (Lewis, various excerpts).

Italian - U.N. Trusteeship Period

Italy's new position in the former colony of Somalia was carefully defined in the United Nations General Assembly on December 2, 1950 (Finkelstein, 3-39). Under the agreement, Italy, in assuming responsibility for the territory was required to develop the region and make recommendations for progress leading to independence in ten years.

The Italian administration practiced indirect rule, that is, it used the existing native institutions and organs of government as part of its system of administration. This approach contributed greatly to the ability of the Somalian people to exercise responsible self-government. The native authorities had the task of maintaining law and order and preventing crimes. They also dealt with the problems of public health, education, and the construction of roads and bridges, water, and the collection of fees. They reported to the Italian administrators through an akil (chief) who was a traditional leader of his tribe and was paid by the central government. The arrangements of the trusteeship also included Advisory Councils, which were formed at the district level in 1951. They were later formed at the divisional level.

These councils were made up of representative Somalis. Their functions ranged from being advisors to the native authorities to having real controlling power according to the situation in each area.

Provisional Government: Transfer of Power to the Somali People

Somalian officials were invited to participate in the work of the administration in 1954 as observers. Abdullah Issa was elected as prime minister of the provisional government when, on February 20, 1956, the First Legislative Assembly was elected. This assembly was given full statutory power in domestic affairs. At this time, the bills adopted by the Assembly were subject to the approval of the Italian Administrator. He could propose legislation to the assembly; he also held the right of absolute veto. In addition, the Italian Administrator could dissolve the assembly and call for new elections within 120 days if he was dissatisfied with its conduct as a legislative body. This body became the governing body of Somalia during independence.

Somalian Independent Government

Somalia became a united, democratic, parliamentary state on July 1, 1960. Tribalism and nepotism were still troubling this young nation. The achievement of unity was handicapped by the poverty of the country since half of each territory's budget was made up of British and Italian subsidies. The modern administration originated from traditional forms, particularly the earlier pastoral democracy. At dependence, 75 percent of the country was still a nomadic society and it emerged from sixty years of colonial rule in an effort to modify its political system into a modern form.

The President of the Republic was the titular Head of State, elected by secret ballot by the members of the National Assembly. For the purposes of election, the Constitution was divided administratively into eight regions and 47 districts, each region headed by a Governor or District Commissioner appointed by the Minister of Interior. Elected units of local government existed only at the municipal level and an elected council and mayor were in charge of the affairs of each population center.

As a final step towards complete self-government, the Executive Branch, the Legislature, and the Judiciary Branch united under the new Somalian Republic. The indigenous government made considerable progress after independence in 1960, in the organization of the government, civil service, reorganization of local government, and concerns of the judicial system.

Coup d'etat of 1969 Scientific Socialism

In 1969, Prime Minister Mohammed Ibrahim was overthrown by a sudden revolutionary change. President Abdi Rashid was assassinated and members of his cabinet were arrested and brought before the popular court for trial and punishment. The legislative body was abolished during all this and the military officers claimed that this was an attempt to clean the country of corruption, tyranny, and foreign influence (Jorunal of Modern Africa Studies, 383-408).

The coup d'etat was partly a result of the widespread corruption in the bureaucratic system that Somalia had inherited from the time of colonization. The civil servants had, according to the revolutionaries, used their positions, not to benefit the people they were supposed to serve, but for their own personal gain (Siad Barre Mohamed, 26-28).

One of the principal goals of the revolutionary government has been to change the political, economic, and social structure of Somali society and to raise the people's standard of living. The bureaucratic system has been entrusted with accelerating the rate of these 'changes and with implementing the programs developed by the new regime (Notes on Somali, 25).

A great deal of emphasis was placed on the idea that public officials are there to serve the needs of the people. Local administration, as an integral part of the State administration, carries out the policy of the state, that is, the construction of a socialist society based on social justice, equality, progress, and unity. According to the first charter issued by the Supreme Revolutionary Council, Scientific Socialism was described as "a society based on the right of work and on principle of social justice considering the environments and social life of the Somali people (Somalia in Transition, 1988)."

Only persons committed to the declared policy of Scientific Socialism and having political consciousness were appointed or selected as members of any council. The Secretary of State of the Interior, under the direction of the Council of Secretaries, supervises the organization and functioning of the local councils. The members of these councils are government employees working in the area as representatives from the local communities.

The Chairman of the Regional Council is the first representative of the central government in the region and is responsible to the President through the Secretary of the Interior. Public administration in Somalia has taken on the role of instilling and perpetuating the ideas and programs of Scientific Socialism.

Further Developments

Somalia is poor in natural resources and faces major developmental problems. It is one of the poorest countries in the world. Its economy is based on livestock and agriculture with scanty and irregular rainfall. Since independence, Somalia has remained nonaligned. It has received aid from the United States, Italy, the Federal Republic of Germany, the Soviet Union, the People's Republic of China, and North Korea. Somalia and Ethiopia have had a border dispute for generations. In the late 1980's the USSR was supporting the Ethiopian government against Somalia by airlifting and selling weapons to Ethiopia. The primary problem facing the administration is that of difficulty with the neighboring country of Ethiopia. As a result, 75 percent of the Somalian budget goes for military defense (African Contemporary Record, 379-380). The conflict with Ethiopia goes beyond both that country and Somalia since both nations depended on aid for their development and arms from the super powers such as the USA and the former USSR. The super powers competed for influence among the nations *in* East Africa. The Somalian Armed Forces previously tended to lean heavily upon Soviet advice and support. *Since* 1969, however, the national military establishment has not relied on Soviet advisors. In recent years, the national administration has established close military relations and cooperation with military advisors from the USA. The United States, after the Soviet Union made a blunder by its support of Ethiopia in the Ethiopian-Somalian conflict, was concerned with helping Somalia build its military and economic strength.

Moscow continued to airlift weapons into Ethiopia and an agreement has been signed for the supply of nearly $800 million worth of Soviet weaponry to Ethiopia (African Contemporary Record, 379-380) Why did Russia opt for Ethiopia? The reason is that Ethiopia was the key to the eventual control of all of Africa. The Soviet goal was to destroy the revolutionary administration of Somalia, which has always had border conflicts with Ethiopia causing a severe strain on the national treasury.

Governmental Structure

The new national administration divided the country into sixteen regions, each containing (except for the capital which has fourteen divisions) three to seven districts (Area Handbook of Somalia, 3). Positions on all district and village councils are held by appointment of the National Government. Hierarchical structure of each council is rigidly observed. The new administration still uses an amalgam of British and Italian legal systems in which Somalian customs still play a small but significant role. Islamic law plays only a formal role in a personal and family sense. Because of these old, traditional policies, and also because of the Ogaden War (the conflict with Ethiopia), which has been absorbing three-fourths of the national budget, it has been almost impossible for these officers to effect sociopolitical-economic reforms which would improve the national standard of living.

Summary

Somalia has suffered from both regional and administrative division since the colonial era. In addition, it is one of the poorest nations in the world, which inherited the colonial system and did not benefit from these alien powers. Furthermore, it has suffered from military administration, an administration usurped from civilians.

Problems Confronting the System

The old traditional style system is still reflected in the present structure, especially the period of colonial rule. Today, the government's major administrative problems are: 1) budgeting and 2) organizing public service. since the power focus today is on military officers, it is very difficult to pinpoint administrative problems. One unit of officers, for example, administers the whole system of the civil service. Because of this fact, the seriousness of the shortage of civil servants has not been evident. Many educated and professional people have left the country through dislike of the military regime. A half million Somalians went to Arab oil-rich countries to work (Africa Contemporary Record, 380). The revolutionary government today still keeps incompetent civil servants on the rolls. The Centre School of Public Administration has been unable to produce high quality, trained people to put in charge of the various divisions of government administration.

What Somalia urgently needs are a well-trained cadre of government administrators, a democratic election with maximum participation to elect a new leader from the people rather than from the armed forces and most importantly, a sufficiently long period of relief from constant border warfare. These are seen as prerequisites to the implementation of social reform.

CHAPTER III

ITALIAN COLONIALISM (1893-1941)

In the late 1800's, Italian administrators, comparing themselves in the world market with those of England and the United States, became concerned with the relative insecurity of Italy's position in international trade. In their search for overseas markets, the Italians began to explore the possibility of the African regions beginning in 1870. More than seventy Italian expeditions were sent to explore Africa.

A flood of expansionist pamphlets and books appeared in general, the expansionist writers specified the need to avoid power struggles, to co-operate with other powers, and to manipulate alliances in order to obtain Overseas benefits. Military conquest was ruled out. If there was to be colonialism, the only possible program would be one calling for peaceful commercial expansion (Hess, 3).

In 1885, when the rules for partition of Africa were set and agreed upon at the Berlin conference, Somalia became open to penetration by European powers. Certain areas of Somalia were considered "no man's land"; areas occupied largely by nomadic Somali tribes who were concerned only with finding adequate pasturage and water for their herds and flocks. On the basis of explorations made by Italian missions, the regions of the Horn of Africa were chosen as potentially new markets, largely because of the navigability of the Juba River which was considered a "natural artery" into the surrounding regions.

During the investigative period, most Somalian trade was being handled by Vincenzo Filonardi, who later became the Italian consul in Zanzibar. The fact that Somalians "hated and feared the Germans gave Italy an unforeseen opportunity to acquire the Somali region at s small cost (Hell, 18).

In September 1893, after intricate and often discouraging negotiations, Filonardi sailed to take possession of the southern region of Somaliland. "A period of cooperative imperialism ended, and a period of colonial government by chartered company began" (Hess, 38).

Nature of Early Colonial System

This period of Filonardi's control was most significant for the lack of control by the central government. Thee Protectorates of northern Somalia were ignored and went their own way most of the time, because the government had no desire to assume financial or military responsibility for them.

This lack of administration by the central government led to feuds and conflicts. On the advice of the head of the Colonial Office, a newly created section of the Italian Ministry of Foreign Affairs, the government granted the Benadir Company provisional administration for six months. In December 1899, this was amended to give continuing control of Somali administration to the Benadir Company.

The Benadir Administration, however, was short-lived; in 1903, reports made to the naval ministry confirmed the suspicions of the Italian government that there was great discontent among the government personnel staff and that the administrative staff was divided into two hostile camps. In 1905, after more such reports, Italy realized that its lack of government responsibility was resulting in irresponsibility on the part of Italian company administrators.

After years of avoiding the issue, the Italian ~ government in 1905 assumed direct administration of Southern Somalia in an effort to create order and peace and a colony out of the wreckage of two disastrous experiments by chartered companies.

Government Organizational Structure

The first set of administrative regulations gave the governor a free hand in the overall direction of the colony and the six adjoining subdivisions of Brava, Merca, Lugh, Itala, Bardera, and Jumbo. For the time being, this oversimplified administration was concerned only with establishing order. In 1908, three years later, a law was passed which united all areas of Southern Somalia under a single administration into Somalia Italiana (Italian Somali land).

This new administration (Italian Somali land) divided the supreme legal power among the Parliament, the metropolitan government, and the colonial government. The civil governor controlled exports, regulated the rate of exchange, raised and/or lowered native taxes, and administered all civil service matters relating to hunting, fishing, and conservation. He was also directly in charge of the colony's police force; he nominated local residents and proposed military arrangements to the metropolitan government; he prepared the annual colonial budget.

Briefly, the law provided for an authoritarian regime that would not have been tolerated in any European country at that time. The new arrangement led to a lack of both discipline and morale. Inasmuch as military men were appointed to civil offices, there was no distinction between the powers of the military and the civil authorities, a situation which led to overt conflicts between Major Antonio de Giorgio, commander of colonial troops and Tomas Carletti, the civil governor, who, needless to say, were in almost constant political conflict--which eventually led to personal disputes.

In 1910, results of investigations into the Somali land administration led the Italian Government to appoint a new governor, G. DeMartino, who was requested by Italy to reconstitute the colonial government.

Basic and important features of DeMartino's new administration were the election of:
1) A civil governor and an executive council composed of a director of civil and political affairs; and
2) A commander of the troops; and the appointment of:
3) Directors for various branches of the government including public works, agriculture, and legal affairs;
4) An accountant.

The above mentioned appointments and newly created departments functioned as follows:
1) The governor was directly responsible to the Colonial Office of the Italian Ministry of Foreign Affairs;
2) The territory was divided into four administrative regions: Upper Juba, Middle Webi Shebelle, Upper Webi Shebelle, and Gosha-Lower Webi Shebelle.

These were further sub-divided into "residencies": Afgoi, Audegle, Salad, Jelib, Margherita, Mahaddei Wen, Matagoi, and
Wanle Wen; in addition to those which had been previously established at Bardera, Brava, Itala, Jumbo, Merca, Meregh,
IDgadishu, and Warsheik.
3) The regional commissioners of the four administrative regions were directly responsible to the governor; the "residents" to the regional commissioner; and the commanders of stations and separate police posts, native chiefs and Muslim cadis (magistrates) administering native law to the "residents"
(Hess, 109)

Personnel System
In the paternalistic vein, a policy of utilizing native personnel was initiated. Chiefs and cadis (juries) were appointed who served as the main points of contact between the central government and· its colonial subjects.

The "residents" submitted annual reports to the regional commissioners regarding the behavior of the chiefs and cadis in a schoolmasterly fashion as "bad, mediocre, good or excellent." The colonial minister very early, was able to report that "with respect to the tribal chiefs of our territory, we can now rely upon their loyalty to the government and upon their performance in the interest of the colony" (Hess, 109) The only restriction placed on the general principles of native law was that they be compatible with the fundamental principles of Italian law.

The overall effect of this personnel system was that it refined original and traditional Somali customs of tribal clan responsibility. The only other area noteworthy of comment during the DeMartino administration (1910-1916) was the creation of a military force under the command of Italian army officers.

After ten years of direct government administration in Southern Somalia, the Italians had created an effective system of indirect rule and had formulated a conservative and practical native policy. They had mitigated the evils of slavery, safeguarded the interior, organized an administrative system and provided for defense and security (Hess, 111).

Economic Development

In the area of economic development of Southern Somaliland, DeMartino was not as successful as he had been in political administration. During the first ten years of direct government administration in Somalia (1910-1920), total trade increased in both imports and exports, thereby increasing customs revenues from zero in 1910 to 4.23 million lire in 1920.

Internal turmoil affected the trade because most of the imports consisted of war material. Although trade picked up after 1912, there was still an unfavorable balance affecting the overall economy because taxable nonmilitary equipment and supplies had to be imported for the newly enlarged staff of the Italian administration. Later on, during the pre-Fascist era (early 1920s) the export trade, consisting mainly of hides and skins, cotton and bananas,began to show some return, which reduced the adverse balance of trade. Yet the colony still ran at a marked deficit and was very far from being the economic asset, which the Italians had predicted (Lewis, 101).

Agriculture

Because investors for agricultural concessions did not come as rapidly and as abundantly as the governor had anticipated, he decided to split up the cultivable land into fifteen different areas and set up a five-year schedule of development with the added incentive of a five-year tax exemption for farmers and concessionaires.

Despite this generous offer of land, it was found that, after the first two years, of the eleven areas in which cultivation had begun, seven had already been abandoned. Again, the governor attempted a new plan, declaring all uncultivated land not used in a permanent fashion by natives to be the property of the state. He also changed the terms of concession by allowing a ten-year tax rebate. In addition, he established an experimental farm and granted loans to concessionaires.

When this second effort also proved unsuccessful, he brought in an agronomist to determine what crops could be profitably grown. The reports of the agronomist, Romola Onor, to the governor were pessimistic, indicating that the natural resources of the colony did not respond to the hopes which superficial affirmations had created.

Among the limiting factors for cultivation noted by the agronomist were: 1) special conditions of soil and climate, 2) irrigation problems, 3) labor supply, and 4) misunderstanding in the farming community regarding the difference between subsistence crops and cash crops.

Referring to this misunderstanding, he said, "If you try to make a native understand that by cultivating cotton with the aid of irrigation, he could have a product worth more than corn, he answers you, 'You can't eat cotton'" (Hess, 115)! In 1919, when hope was given up for agricultural development, the Duke of Abruzzi, an explorer, became interested in the agricultural possibilities of the East African regions and began a highly mechanized commercial plantation on the middle Webi Shebelle in South Somaliland.

The then governor Rivieri who was eager for the economic development to begin called for quick government action to subsidize this undertaking. After intensive technical research, the Shebelle rapidly developed into a highly efficient agricultural consortium producing cotton, sugar, bananas, oil, and soap.

In large measure the success of this enterprise was due not only to the organizing genius of its founder, and to the rational scientific preparation which preceded each phase of the work, but also to the strenuous efforts which were made to overcome the traditional difficulties of labour recruitment (Lewis, 93).

This venture called Societa Agficola Italo-Somala, (S.A.I.S.) which proved to be a well-timed development had many far reaching effects. A new system of land sharing and title contract was formed which benefited the local tribesmen, especially the Bantu Shidle amongst whom the consortium was established.

The long neglected site of Onor, the agronomist's pioneering research station--a vast irrigation project for plantation cultivation--was reopened. A new wage system was devised whereby the farmer earned both seed for new crops as well as money. Last, but not least, was the economical effect on the territory. The export of bananas soon became the main object of production. Production of sugar and cotton increased and the bulk of these were exported. Corresponding developments arose in other fields, particularly in communications. Roads were extended or new ones built and a small diesel railway system was established linking the plantations for easy access. The first government geological survey was initiated to provide the basis for a badly needed well-drilling scheme to aid the nomadic sector of the economy. Social services in the area of hospitals and schools began and a school for training of hospital orderlies was opened in 1933.

Financial System

There was no cash money system of finance during the early Colonial administration. An attempt was made at currency reform by the colonial government but this was not successful because the Somalis would not accept paper money. It was not until after World War I that the introduction of a metropolitan currency was adopted.

The only notable area in the area of finances was in the field of taxation. This occurred during the Fascist Period of Governor C.M. DeVecchi di Val Cismon, from 1923 to 1928. By 1941, after many years of border conflicts and outright warfare, Italy expanded her territory into the northern protectorate by agreement with the British.

The same type of administration, which existed at that time in the Southern Region, was applied there, except that it was not a peaceable transition of government.

There was the ever-present and still-going-strong border conflict with Ethiopia and together with world depression, it was a trying time for both Somali natives and Italian administrators. Taxation was a direct result of the rule-by-force Fascist regime. In order to meet the colony's increasing budget, the then Governor DeVecchi imposed the first direct tax on the Somalis.

This was, on the whole, successful and the revenue was more than doubled in the pre-1926 period (Hess, 160).

Because of the success of this venture, additional taxes were levied on the community; there was a 1 to 5 per cent tax on net business incomes, in addition to rents and a personal income tax on a graduated scale. The personal income tax was not consistent to any particular form, because only sections of the community, for example, bachelors who lived in the towns, and unmarried male Italians between the ages of twenty-five and sixty-five, had to pay this tax. Even so, most revenue still came largely from customs receipts. With growing world depression from 1930 to 1934, the drop in worldwide income reflected in Somalia's declining export trade. To meet this decline in revenue, taxes were increased.

Outcome and Problems of the Colonial Period

The most significant feature of the colonial period of administration was during the rule of Governor G. DeMartino from 1910 to 1916. The governor realized the importance of combining indirect rule with paternalism. He showed himself sensitive to the needs of the Somali people and also realized that this was the best way to achieve results at the smallest cost. It is therefore not difficult to understand why this system of, administration lasted until 1941 - the longest period of any single administrative system in Somalia's history.

Because of underdevelopment, Somaliland was far from being self-sufficient at the end of the Italian Colonial period. It is thought that had it not been for the war and its own internal conflicts, more attention would have been paid to its agricultural development.

Failure of the central administration during the colonialist period was due in part to the fact that although the Italians preserved--for their own purposes--the chieftainship system, they never completely understood or studied the system and therefore were unaware of many aspects of their own governmental units.

The constant border conflicts did not, in any way, help the administration. However, in concentrating their efforts on these border conflicts, the Italian administrators did not realize that internally, the Somali clans and tribes did not all follow the same beliefs and customs which led to internal clashes.

Somalia was considered an economic burden by Italy and even though few changes were made in Somalia's education system and in its social organizations, Somalians were acutely aware of a way of life different from the tribal existence with which they were familiar. This period of Italian rule made the tribes realize that their traditional tribal system was useless in a modern society.

The primary obstacle in organizing for rapid social and economic change in contemporary Somalia is not found in indigenous traditions, but rather in the inherited colonial institutions.

A serious threat to the undemocratic system of indirect rule comes from those Somali who had become Europeanized. When the young men who had left their tribal organizations to work with Europeans or those who had received higher education returned to their homes, they often challenged the tribal "authorities" sanctioned *by* the colonial system. These young men who had observed modern administrative procedures or who had become acquainted with modern labor and political movements frequently endeavored to initiate programs designed to democratize their tribal government.

CHAPTER IV
SOMALILAND: UNDER ITALIAN ADMINISTRATION
(1950-1960)

Years Preceding Trusteeship (1940-1950)
British Military Administration

Compared with previous and future systems of administration, the British Military occupation of Somalia from 1940 to 1950 was not significant in terms of structure or economic development. Only a brief description will be given here in order to link the period of transition from the Italian Colonialism to Italian Trusteeship, highlighting the main points during these ten years of British Military Administration.

The British were well received, since they were looked upon as liberators from the previous Fascist era. After almost twenty years of Fascist rule, the Somalians were ready and willing to accept the removal of restrictions, which had been placed on them. Even the fact that British law was strictly enforced gained the respect of the Somalians, inasmuch as this was seen as a necessary part of advancement of cultural and social conditions.

This could be described as the period of Somali unification. The most significant effect during this period was in the mood and outlook of the Somalians, who were either getting used to changes in system and therefore were complacent about the British occupation or were getting so disgusted that they were ready for revolt.

The Somalians were becoming increasingly motivated towards future independence and looked for changes in structure to hasten this movement. Among radical and sweeping changes made during British occupation were: 1) disbandment of the previous Italian (Fascist) police force which was replaced by a hastily recruited Somalian Gendarmerie under British officers; 2) replacement of Italian provincial administration (which had collapsed during the Walwal fighting) in all provinces and districts by placing them in charge of British Civil Affairs officers; 3) encouragement of tribal assemblies and these new councils in turn were encouraged to deal with local problems of water supplies, agricultural improvement, unemployment and food scarcity (Lewis, 118).

Modest but realistic advances were made in the field of education. Towards the end of 1947, the Italians began a "direct and forthright propaganda campaign" for the return of Somalia to Italy. Tensions mounted as disputes and conflicts increased until Britain and Italy were engaged in full-scale conflict resulting in an atmosphere of tension and animosity.

During all this, the ever-present Ethiopia tried to intervene so that Somalia would become united with Ethiopia, not necessarily because Ethiopia had suddenly become friendly, but because their previous experiences with Italy, especially in the Walwal incident, were far from rewarding, and they did not wish to see Somalia back in Italian hands.

It was at this stage that the United Nations intervened and began making arrangements to make Somaliland a trustee nation under Italian administration and with the important condition that the country become independent in ten years.

United Nations-Italian Trusteeship Agreement

The Somalians benefitted from the experience of self-rule which was encouraged during British occupation from 1940 to 1950 and with this new political knowledge, in addition to their traditional "democratic pastoral social system," they felt themselves ready to prepare for independence. The United Nations Assembly, on December 2, 1950 drew up an agreement for a period of ten years, in which the Somalis would be further educated politically under Italian trusteeship.

Italy's new position in her former colony of Somalia was carefully and closely defined in the United Nations Trusteeship Agreement ... to foster the development of free political institutions and to promote the developments of the inhabitants of the territory towards independence (Lewis, 139).

To achieve this end, Somalis were to be given increasing responsibility in the political and administrative control of their country with the assistance of the Italian

Government and under the guidance of the United Nations.

In order to make sure that the Italians fulfill their responsibility of trust, a special U.S. Advisory Council was created to provide direct liaison with the Italian Administration and its wards. As seen at that time, the problem in brief was to create indigenous organs of government and administration, which would meet the needs of an independent state. To all parties concerned, it was apparent that economic viability would be almost impossible to achieve in ten years, therefore the idea was to find ways of improving services, at the same time reducing the revenue deficit, which was seen as the greatest obstacle towards self-government.

This problem, which would have been difficult enough to overcome, was further complicated by:

a. The felt necessity not to undertake capital ventures which would impose added burdens on the budget of an independent Somalia; and

b. The special limitations imposed on the import trade, both of capital and personnel, by the ten-year period with its attendant uncertainties (Finkelstein, 5).

Nature of the System Under Trusteeship

Education

The new system designed for rapid development began appropriately in the field of education. This took the form of an "ambitious and imaginative" scheme for a five-year development program instituted in 1952 with UNESCO collaboration. Primary and secondary schools, technical institutes, and higher educational programs were set up. Further measures were taken to arrange for study overseas. Attempts were made for a program of adult education for the nomadic population but this proved unsuccessful (Lewis, 140).

Political System

Political advancement proceeded step by step with the
replacement of the Italians by Somalian officials in the civil
service and police force. This resulted in a smooth transition of
authority in both administrative and political spheres with the
same pace of advancement. A further step was taken in this
direction when the Advisory Council suggested that legislative
Advisory committees and offices be created to prepare the way
for fuller delegation of political authority. In 1956, when Somalis
were "replacing Italians in all senior administrative positions,
these developments further enhanced by the transformation of the
Territorial Council into a Legislative Assembly. This new
Assembly was given full statutory powers in domestic affairs
although the head of the Italian Trust Administration retained the
right of absolute veto.

Elections, with suffrage confined to men, were held and
whatever shortcomings may have marred the conduct of the
elections in the rural areas, the exuberance with which the
general population seized this first opportunity to express its
political will was remarkable (Lewis, 146).

Finance and Economic system

With an annual subsidy of over three million pounds from Italy
(Lewis, 142), much of this was needed for reconstruction and
repair: improved roads, communications, public works in the
areas of health, education and the newly formed government
administration.

On the whole, Somalia remained desperately poor and
continued to run at a serious deficit. While local revenue derived
principally from import and export dues were doubled, and
expenditures were decreased, there was still a considerable
adverse balance of payments (Lewis, 142).

The general economic picture was such that the World
Bank Mission which visited the territory in 1957 realized that
financial assistance would be required for at least twenty years
after independence. Overall, the nature of the system was
designed for rapid changes in all areas of administration with

interest naturally centered on the internal issues of vital concern to the future stability and prosperity of the state.

Importance was also placed on an effort to settle the disputed frontier of Ethiopia. In the last years of the trusteeship, the Government was preoccupied with the important question of preparing a constitution for independence. To this end, two committees were set up to study the problem. A political committee was concerned with the overall structure of the new administration and a technical committee was responsible for drafting the principles of this constitution. It was explained that in drafting the constitution, priority should be placed on unification of the Somali territories.

The Somali form a single race, practices the same religion and speak a single language. They inhabit a vast territory, which, in its turn, constitutes a well-defined geographic unit. All must know that the government of Somalia will strive its uttermost, with the legal and peaceful means which are its democratic prerogative to attain this end; the union of Somalia, until all Somalis form a single Greater Somalia (Lewis, 161)

Organizational Structure and Program Development Under Trusteeship

In discussing the organizational structure of the government under the trusteeship administration, instead of using the Terms of Agreement (See Appendix III) which stated what was to be done in areas of reorganization, we will look at what had been accomplished. The following account will be comprised of excerpts taken from a report issued by the United Nations Visiting Mission to Somaliland in 1957, after seven years of Italian Trusteeship Administration and two years before the country gained its independence. We will therefore be concerned chiefly with the results of this trusteeship arrangement and then present system of organization.

Constitutional Development and Political' Advancement:

The Administering Authority in 1956 granted a large measure of autonomy to the inhabitants of the Territory. An elective

Legislative Assembly and a cabinet system of government consisting of a Prime Minister at the head of a Council of Ministers was established. The administration of all regions and districts had been entrusted to Somali civil servants in 1955 and an increasing number of senior posts in the administrative services had been filled by Somalis.

The government of Somalia was vested with wide powers with regard to the internal administration of the Territory, and any limitations on its authority which still existed pertained mainly to the responsibilities of the Administering Authority in external affairs. An increasing number of Somali civil servants were receiving training in the diplomatic field. The Administering Authority continued to hold powers in relation to defense and public order. The military and police forces had been merged into the Somalia Police Force, which was divided into territorial and mobile corps, the latter composed almost entirely of motorized units. The territorial corps was under the authority of the Minister of Internal Affairs, whereas the mobile corps together with an Italian armored force remained under the Administrator's control. It was envisioned that within a short time, both the mobile units and the armored force would be placed under Somali command.

On the civil side of the administration, although Somalian personnel were replacing Italians in some of the higher posts, the Italians agreed to remain entirely at the disposal of the Somalian government until qualified staff became available.

Educational Advancement

Technical and teacher training schools and a police academy had been opened and intensive educational programs were instituted among Somalis enrolled in the military forces. In Mogadishu, a School of Public Administration was created with an ever-increasing enrollment. Graduates of the school had been sent to Italy for further study at the Somalia Study Center; these students, when they returned took up places in the Administration. Other established institutions were the Higher Institute of Legal, Economic and Social Studies and an increased number of elementary and secondary institutions.

Two serious problems in the area of education addressed by these reforms were: 1) shortage of teaching personnel; and 2) lack of a written form of the Somali language. The United Nations Visiting Mission in 1957 was critical of the Administration's policies with respect to education. Its criticism concerned three points: One was the absence of education for the nomads, which led the Mission to recommend the establishment of experimental schools. A second was the lack of secondary and technical schools outside Mogadishu. Thirdly, the Mission was concerned over the lack of efforts to train Somalis for the assumption of responsibilities in the administration (UN Visiting Mission 1957).

Economic Development' Under Trusteeship

The United Nations Visiting Mission in 1957 reported on economic development that without continuing financial aid after 1960 there would be a drastic reduction in present standards of administration, education and the social services and the frustration of hopes for higher living standards in the future drastic cuts in public expenditures and imports would have to be planned right away and investment plans curtailed (UN Visiting Mission 1957, 11).

On this issue of economic development and revenue deficit, the United Nations Visiting Mission and the Administering Authority did not agree. The Administering Authority informed the Council that while it shared the conclusions in the report it considered that certain of these were somewhat pessimistic, especially in regard to banana production costs and the outlook for exporting bananas at a competitive price. The Government of Italy was resolved to continue this kind of assistance after' 1960 to the extent that the Government of Somalia asked for it. It also expressed the hope that the United Nations would provide technical assistance (UN Visiting Mission 1957, 11).

The Prime Minister requested that the United Nations assist the Somalis in solving its economic problems because he realized the enormity of the problem of continuing revenue deficit. He stressed the urgency of obtaining an assurance well beforehand of the external aid the Territory would receive after independence so as to permit the drawing up of plans for that period. The Prime Minister also stressed the willingness and desire of the Somali people to contribute to the development of their country in order to improve the standard of living of the farming and pastoral population.

Financial System

The financial system inherited many problems, among them a substantial budget deficit and a lack of trained personnel to effectively administer the processes of planning, policy analysis, and development. These can be seen as key factors in the weakness of national efforts to build a strong economy. These difficulties were further compounded by the many problems arising from the food and energy crises, the effects of which were apparent in inflation and monetary disturbances.

The budgetary system had no central role in the trustee process and therefore had no real opportunity for improvement. The role of planning was diminished to advisory functions and therefore alienated the budgeting system from the total administration. No attempt was made to provide an adequate base for efficient budgeting and elaboration of the annual financial reports, which are normally done during the planning process. It is with respect to the costing of major projects that the record of planning has led to usually poor developmental plans, which would normally provide a rough and broad magnitude of overall costs.

This lack of a comprehensive and unified financial system led to impaired and sometimes constrained implementation of the financial process. There were no wide range financial institutions existing in the Trustee Administration such as commercial banks, governmental agencies, etc., which could provide banking services. The post office remained the major bank sources for the population and there was an obvious lack of banking systems, which could identify, formulate and promote specific investment projects or provide support services such as provision of managerial training in this capacity.

Institution of a banking system should have been encouraged to participate in the programs and activities relating to development of small scale agricultural industries which would have had a durable impact on the development of a credit system for the purpose of essential imports and support for marketing of products.

With this issue left undefined, there was a communication breakdown between the planning authority and the budgeting authority and any programs and policies that had any meaning were necessarily stifled by loss of control over performance results in terms of planned targets and projected program outcomes (UN Visiting Mission 1957, 18,).

Transition of Authority

In December 1959, the United Nations General Assembly adopted a resolution determining that Somalia's trusteeship should terminate on July 1, 1960. The British Protectorate, which was to join the Southern Italian Province to complete the unification of Somalia, was opposed to the date set because some of the issues between the Italians and the British had not yet been resolved.

The United Nations would not back down on the date, resulting in a last mad rush of political activity to settle differences in policy. The Protectorate leaders met in London in May 1960 at the conference which was to sever their colonial connections with Somalia and finally came to an agreement because the main objective was the same for both nations: that all responsibility be relinquished; their own arguments of regional distribution were no longer applicable.

CHAPTER V

SOMALI REPUBLIC (1960-1969)

Somalia, which became a "unitary, democratic, parliamentary" state on July 1, 1960, emerged from over 60 years of colonial rule with its political tradition not destroyed, but rather unified, revitalized and channeled into modern forms. The common bond of Islam contributed strongly to this unity.

The colonizing powers had little or no economic interest in the country other than in the limited agricultural development. The numerous and rapid changes of administration which expanded and contracted, appeared, disappeared and reappeared constituted, on the whole, in a more unified Somalia with its inherent traditionalism making way for its independence. This period of independence continued until 1969 when the parliamentary government was replaced by a socialist government.

Nature of the System - National Level

The Constitution of the new Republic called for the formation of a National Assembly - a multiparty body -, which became the real center of political power in the state. The Constitution also declared the official religion of Islam to be the main source of its laws (Legum, 187).

National Assembly

The size of the Assembly was not constitutionally limited but at independence, consisted of 123 members, 33 from the Northern Region (former British Somali land) and 90 from the Southern Region (the former Trust Territory), all elected by popular vote (Legum, 188).

The Assembly sat for a term of five years unless dissolved sooner by the President of the Republic. There were two fixed annual sessions in April and October. Other sessions were held on demand of the President, the Council of Ministers or of one-fourth of the deputies (Legum, 188)

The president and vice-president of the National Assembly were elected by deputies from within their own membership which was divided into committees and subcommittees for the purpose of drafting legislation. These deputies were representatives of their own parties and groups.

The first act of the Assembly was to elect a new president, Aden Abdulla Osman. The President, in turn, selected a prime minister, who then had to obtain the vote of confidence from the National Assembly within 30 days of selection. The new president was elected on June 20, 1961, but his election was made retroactive as of the date of independence in July 1960. The Constitution called for the President of the New Republic to be the titular head of state, but not the executive head of government. According to the terms of the Constitution, he was representative of national unity and as the chief mediator in times of government crisis, he wields considerable power. As chief of state his honorific duties include the accrediting and receiving of diplomatic representatives. He is the commander of the armed forces. All legislation and treaties must bear his signature. Draft legislation and government messages to the National Assembly also must be signed by him, but in all of these acts he functions on behalf of the prime minister (Legum, 190).

The president's only real power was exercised when he was required to pick a new prime minister, either after governmental crisis or at the time of the election of a new National Assembly. Even so, he was bound to choose a candidate who had the support of the majority party in the legislature.

The Constitution also provided for the complete independence of the judiciary. The highest court, the Supreme Court, with the addition of four extra members - two appointed by the Council of Ministers and two elected by the National Assembly - functioned as a Constitutional Court.

The Constitutional Court, unlike the courts in many systems, decided on the conformity of legislation to the provisions of the Constitution and to the principles of Islam. The Supreme Court of Somalia also adjudicated election disputes and served as a High Court of Justice to hear impeachment cases.

Nature of the System – Local Level

Because of the long and narrow shape of the territory (see map on page 73), the absence of railroads presented a communication problem, which was early, recognized by the government leaders and administrators of the new Somali Republic. It became especially important that local authorities should be able to run their own affairs without depending too heavily on the central government. Because of this fact, it was decided to retain the pre-independence system of regional government. In this connection, the Local Administration and Local Council Elections Law of 1963 was passed which promoted decentralization and self-government by encouraging local authorities to assume greater responsibilities (Harris, 23).

In preparation of this law, a study was made of the Northern and Southern systems of local administration, which revealed major differences between the two systems. In the South, the jurisdiction of the municipalities was confined to urban centers, whereas in the North the jurisdiction of Local Councils extended also to the rural areas. In the South, all the councilors were elected; in the North, some were elected and others appointed. In the integrated law of 1963, the Northern system was adopted and the whole territory of the Republic was placed under the jurisdiction of local administrators.

This decision was explained as follows:

It is considered essential that all citizens, including those living in isolated sections, should be able to look upon a local administration as the authority responsible for providing the essential services. The abolition of any distinction between urban and rural areas should prevent neglect for the sections of the Territory most distant from the main urban centres. At the same time, it should give the inhabitants of those sections a feeling of more direct participation in local government (Report on Local Administration, 23).

As in the pre-independence system of government, regional governors, district commissioners, and district delegates were charged with supervising public order in their respective districts. Some of their other duties included issuing of licenses and land leases.

Government Organization Structure – National Level

The Republic of Somalia during independence from 1960 to 1969, was headed by a National Assembly, which consisted of 123 members, all popularly elected. The President of the Republic was elected by secret ballot of the National Assembly and the President in turn, selected a Prime Minister who was appointed after obtaining a vote of confidence from the National Assembly.

Executive functions were exercised by the government, composed of the prime minister and his subordinate ministers who sat together under" his chairmanship as the Council of Ministers. The prime minister and the Council of Ministers, not the president of the republic, were responsible to the National Assembly for the acts of the government, even though the President signed them. The Council of Ministers were appointed by the president on recommendation by the prime minister, who made the actual decisions. The prime minister also selected, with the assistance of his ministers, a number of undersecretaries of state to act as assistants to the minister. The size of the Council of Ministers was not specified in the Constitution and therefore varied from one government to another.

The president of the republic and the Council of Ministers utilized separate secretariats. The president's secretariat was called the Office of the Presidency; that of the Council of Ministers was called the Presidency of the Council of Ministers, which included a cabinet and was the office of the executive staff of the Council (Report of Interregional Seminar, 30).

Organization of Government Ministries

The administrative official in each ministry was its director general, an official selected by the minister and appointed by presidential decree. His office was called the General Direction and in the larger ministries was divided into separate departments, each with its own departmental head. For example, the Ministry of Finance was divided into Fiscal, Accounting, and State Domain Departments. These divisions were called sections, services and offices.

The Office of the Magistrate of Accounts and the Judiciary, which included the Office of the General Prosecutor, did not come under the government or any or its ministries. Several other organs of the government were semi-independent of the control of the minister, such as the National Bank of Somali, the Somali Port Authority and the Social Insurance Fund. There were also a number of interministerial committees the most important of which was the National Security Council composed of the prime minister; the ministers of interior, foreign affairs, and defense; and the commander of the national army and the national police (Report on the Development of Senior Administrators 1968, 31).

Government Organization Structure – Local Level

The Constitution directed that, whenever possible, administrative functions were to be decentralized. Because of this and the pre-independence division of the country, the ministries adopted the same geographical subdivisions called regions.

There were eight formal major administrative and political regions. These were further divided into 47 districts, six of which had one or two sub districts. Each region had a regional governor; each district, a district commissioner and the sub districts, a district delegate; all coming under the minister of the interior. Groups elected local representatives and they served as channels through which both directives were communicated downward and political and welfare demands of the populace were passed upward.

Municipal Government:

In addition to the regional and district divisions, there were approximately 58 municipalities with elected governments. The municipal council consisted of from 11 to 25 councilors, depending upon the population and was elected by popular vote for a four-year term.

These councilors in turn elected one of their number as mayor and another as deputy mayor, both for two-year terms. The minister of the interior maintained supervisory control over the operations of the municipalities and had the power to remove mayors and deputies. In some matters, e.g. granting of long-term land leases, the decisions of the municipal council required the approval of either the regional governor or the district commissioner. The elected officials of each municipal council were assisted by administrative officers who were civil servants trained in local government affairs. They were appointed by the regional governor and were responsible to the governor (Report on Development of Senior administrators, 31).

Personnel System

The personnel administration system was governed d ring independence by Civil Service Law No. 7 of 5 March 962, which was extremely rigid and concentrated all administrative powers in the hands of higher authorities, the President of the Republic and the Council of Ministers.

This law divided civil service posts into four grades: A, B, C, and D with D being the lowest rank. The appointment, promotion and transfer of all civil servants were made by a "decree of the President of the Republic on the proposal of the competent minister, approved by the Council of Ministers"{Article 14).

Entrance to the government service was through open competitive examination with a probationary period after appointment of six months to one year. The law also provided for the submission of annual confidential reports in which judgment was passed upon the efficiency, performance and conduct of officers.

Most senior administrators had no university education and were for that reason deprived of a great deal of modern knowledge, which is indispensable for efficient administrative performance. There was also a lack of practically experienced individuals who were needed for higher policy decision making.

The Somali Institute of Public Administration instituted training programs for public servants in various levels of the public service with special emphasis on the training of middle-level management personnel. Some of their special seminars included: "What went wrong with our five-year plan" and "Administrative obstacles to development" (1962 Manual on Duties and Responsibilities).

Finance System and Economic Development

In tackling the severe economic and financial situation in independent Somalia, the government was faced with the first problem of planning to include the finance system into the overall administrative structure.

Budget

Before 1966, the Central Government operated an ordinary budget and a special budget covering development projects wholly or partly financed by the Somali Government. Beginning in 1966, all central government transactions were integrated into one budget while development expenditures financed by official foreign sources were not included in the budget.

The central government budget for 1967, which included the regional governments, provided for total expenditures of 272 million Somali shilling, exceeding estimated revenues by 24 million Somali shilling (Surveys of African Economies, 386). The municipalities were generally self-financing with revenue sources available from house and land taxes, license fees on trades and professions, taxes on livestock sales and surtax on the central government income tax. The Ministry of Public Works also contributed to the budgets of the municipalities for the execution of projects.

Banking

Somalia's banking system was comprised of a central bank - the Somali National Bank and five commercial banks, four of which were branches of foreign banks. Credito Somalo, the only Somaliowned commercial bank, operated a development loan section, which extended medium-term and long-term development credit.

Since 1963, the Somali National Bank has increased its commercial banking and later in 1967, when services became automated, increased its functions both locally and internationally, by credit expansion through membership as a representative of Somalia in the International Monetary Fund (1966 Somali National Bank Director's Report).

On August 31, 1962, Somalia joined the International Monetary Fund and its quota as at September 1, 1968 was $15,000,000. On the same day, it joined the International Bank for Reconstruction and Development (World Bank) and its subscription as at September 1, 1968 was also $15,000,000. Other subscriptions included the International Development Association at $760,000 and the International Finance Corporation at $83,000 (Surveys of African Economies, 366).

Economic Development

Because of the absence of adequate and reliable data on domestic production, it is difficult to estimate the pace and pattern of the economic development during the years of independence (1960-1969). Reliance therefore has to be placed on the identifiable economic indicators such as banana production and exports, livestock exports, investment expenditures, and fiscal and credit developments. (See Appendix V for Economic and Financial Indicators after implementation of Five-Year Program).

In order to promote the expansion of agricultural production, the government established an Agricultural Development Agency in February 1966. Its primary functions were to extend farm credit, consolidate small and inefficient holdings into larger units, and foster agricultural cooperatives. Both technical and financial assistance was provided by the United Nations. Somalia's first Five-Year Development Plan was initiated in 1963 (1963-1967). An appraisal of the plan in 1966 proved that implementation had lagged considerably behind target. These delays were due mainly to the absence of effective coordination, a result of a shortage of skilled administrative and trained personnel.

Outcome

The Somalian independent system of government began having problems only two years after the new administration had been in force. In 1962, disagreements arose between the heads of state as to priorities. The Prime Minister felt that unification of all Somali populated territories should be the issue dominating Somali politics because of their border disputes; the President felt that internal economic and social problems should first be attended to.

This disagreement came to a head during the 1964 elections when the President chose to ignore the results of the vote, and even went as far as expelling party officials who had voted against him. As a result of this expulsion, his cabinet ministers resigned in protest and this governmental crisis left Somalia ungoverned from February to September of 1964. On September 27, 1964, a new cabinet was chosen which was satisfactory to the leading party and which remained in effect until the presidential elections in June 1967.

The Republic of Somalia, in addition to its inherited problems of *economic* stability and an overcentralized system of government, created problems for itself when the Republic *in* 1963 refused an offer of military assistance valued at almost *six* and a half million pounds from the West in favor of Russian *mili*tary aid *in* the amount of nearly eleven million pounds (Lewis, 210). This move was seen as representing a definite change of direction in Somalia's political history. Border dispute with Ethiopia was also causing problems to the new nation and *in* 1968 when Somali's anger and despair showed over Britain's siding with Ethiopia *in* one of the many clashes between Somalia and Ethiopia, the People's Republic of China intervened and offered support. Previous to this, trade and aid agreements had been signed by China and Somalia and it seemed likely that Somalia would lean towards Communism.

In October 1969, the President of the Republic was assassinated and six days later, power was seized by army commanders led by Commander-in-Chief, Maj. Gen. Mohamed Siad Barre, supported by the police. The 1960 Constitution was suspended and a new government was formed by a Supreme Revolutionary Council, which proclaimed the Somali Democratic Republic.

One year later, on the anniversary of the revolution in October, President Barre declared Somalia a socialist state and began a revolutionary program of national unification and social and economic reform.

CHAPTER VI

SOMALI DEMOCRATIC REPUBLIC (1969-1991)

The Somali Democratic Republic is the governmental system that prevailed in Somalia until 1991. The first acts of the Supreme Revolutionary Council (SRC) in October 1969 were to:

> dissolve the National Assembly and dismiss its deputies, and to abolish the Supreme Court and place under arrest or restriction all members of the previous government. They then changed the name of the Somali Republic to the Somali Democratic Republic and issued their first charter, which stated their basic aims.

These were to:
- Constitute a society based on the right to work and on principle of social justice considering the environments and social life of the Somali people;
- Prepare and orient the development of economic, social and cultural programs to reach a rapid progress of the country;
- Liquidate illiteracy and develop an enlightened patrimonial and cultural heritage of the Somali people
- Constitute, with appropriate and adequate measures, the basic development of the writing of the Somali language;
- Liquidate all kinds of corruption, all forms of anarchy, the malicious system of tribalism in every form and every phenomena of bad customs in state activities; and
- Abolish all political parties, and to conduct at appropriate time free and impartial elections.

The second charter issued one year later declared Scientific Socialism as the "cherished goal of the Somali Democratic Republic" and that "socialism is the only philosophical system that can establish a society based on labour and the principles of social justice (Europa Year Book, 1359)."

Nature of the System

Having declared the intention of establishing a socialist society in Somalia, the government took significant steps toward creating and strengthening the institutional framework with basic administrative changes. The aim of the new system was to orient the administrative system to the principles of socio-political philosophy of scientific socialism and to reinforce the administrative capacity of the country for planning programs leading to economic development.

The system was based on the following changes:

1. To state the major areas of deficiency in the administrative system;
2. To make basic administrative reforms;
3. To improve personnel administration and manpower with a view to constructive planning;
4. To improve the financial system of administration; and
5. To promote research and exchange of information with ways of increasing economic development (Journal of Modern Africa Studies, 64).

The system was geared towards rapid economic and social transformation and a very high priority was placed on programs of national guidance and political orientation of the population. Members of the Somali Revolutionary Council, through mass meetings, explained the aims of socialism and the need for radical changes in their attitudes and beliefs. In order to continue this program of orientation, centers were established throughout the country and lectures and visual presentations on socialism were presented. These centers became gathering places for the common people living near these centers. A new system of filing was devised and recommended for all ministries. Draft regulations on financial and accounting procedures for public agencies were prepared and submitted to the Government of Somalia. A revised system of accounting for agricultural development was prepared and miscellaneous assignments were completed and used for improvement of the Office of the

Magistrate of Accounts, the Ministry of Justice and Religious Affairs, the Ministry of Finance and the Somali Insurance Company.

A new system of civil service recruitment and training was established with the emphasis being placed on the dynamic role of the public servant in building a socialist system. Perhaps the most important single factor in the changed system was the tremendous self-help activity through voluntary labor and material contributions going on allover the country, from the cleaning of village streets to construction of roads (Knezevic, SOM 78/008).

Government Organization Structure

On October 27, 1969, one week after the coup the Supreme Revolutionary Council, chaired by Siad Barre, appointed a 14 member predominantly civilian cabinet to run the day-to-day administration with the promise that the next general elections to be held in March 1970, would be conducted fairly. In December 1974, the Supreme Revolutionary Council was reorganized into five committees to deal with social, political and economic affairs, the judiciary, and security. In July 1976, the SRC dissolved itself and power was transferred to the newly formed Somali Revolutionary Socialist Party (SRSP); all members of the SRC became members of the ruling party's Central Committee (Europa Year Book, 1359).

Under the draft constitution prepared by the Supreme Revolutionary Council, the president and Council have all governmental powers including those of the former National Assembly. When the SRC was dissolved and replaced by the Supreme Revolutionary Socialist Party, the President of the Republic became also the SRSP's Secretary-General and he directed the government with the assistance of an appointed Council of Ministers.

The Somali Institute of Public Administration played a significant role in the new administration when they were asked to submit recommendations for change in the structure of the government with a view to the main goal of achieving Scientific

Socialism. Because the Supreme Revolutionary Council in making the necessary changes adopted these recommendations, this handbook will be used as the basic source of information in describing the organizational structure except as further noted (Area Handbook presented to the Supreme Revolutionary Council).

Executive Powers

The Supreme Revolutionary Council is the highest decision-making and control organ in the country of Somalia. It comprises a President who represents the unity of the country and also performs the functions of Head of State; three Vice-Presidents and seventeen members, all appointed by the President to form a cabinet. Decisions are made on a collective basis.

Besides participating in the decision-making process, the SRC members perform executive functions mainly as:

- Members of SRC Committees;
- Advisers to the President;
- Secretaries of State for the Ministries; and
- Managers of Public Agencies.

Top-level coordination and control is provided by this body (Area Handbook presented to SRC).

Local Government

With a view to decentralizing government authority on the basis of principles of a socialist democracy, fundamental legislation was passed regarding local government reforms. Until 1973, the country was divided into eight regions, each headed by an official chosen by the central government. The regions were subdivided into 47 districts, headed by district commissioners also appointed by the government.

There were 83 municipalities and submunicipalities. The powers of the municipal councils included local taxation, town planning, registry and census, public services, and approval of the local budget.

The major educational, economic, and social services were financed and maintained by the central government, which also exerted supervisory control over the municipal councils through its power to remove mayors and to dissolve the councils. In 1973, local government reorganization raised the number of regions from 8 to 14 and established the city of Mogadisho as a separate governmental entity. All regional and district officials are now chosen by the SRC although some village councils have some elected officials.

The Chairman of the Regional Council is responsible to the President of the Supreme Revolutionary Council through the Secretary of the Interior. The Chairman of the District Council is local supervisor of all public servants in the district, responsible to the regional council and its chairman. Regional and district development plans will be in keeping with national goals under the supervision of the *Ministry* of 7 Finance and incorporation in the State budget (Europa Year Book, 1359).

Financial Administration

A number of important developments were made in the area of financial administration particularly in the areas of budgeting, expenditure control, audit control and finances of public agencies.

A procedure for Plan-Budget Coordination was established with a more objective definition of annual plan targets. The annual budget was extended to include foreign aid and loans. The overall financial system was unified to include the budgets of municipal, district and regional administrations and public agencies in the central budget. This was done in order to strengthen central control over the mobilization and allocation of resources.

For the first time in the history of the country the Government budget was balanced, so that in 1970 a surplus of 16.9 million Somali Shillings appeared. The government mobilized internal resources, increased economy in ordinary budget expenses and also increased internal resources for development expenditure. By 1973, the new scope of the government budget expanded to cover the public agencies and enterprises as well as resources of the regional and district councils (Somalia: Economic Development, 23).

In the 1980-1988 period, two crises adversely affected the stability of the budget. These were:

1) The disastrous drought, which hit the country in 1977 and lasted throughout 1988 affecting agricultural production. The government had to dislocate all resources to help the people stricken by the drought,

2) The border dispute in Ogaden in 1978, which, because of increased military spending, caused a deficit in the budget for the first time since 1970. This 1978 deficit amounted to 22 million Somali Shillings.

External assistance played a very important role during this period, due to the following factors:
1) Financing of the current budget deficit;
2) Financing of development plans;
3) Financing deficits in balance of payments
4) Financing of the drought stricken people after the 1973-1975 drought; and
5) Financing of relief of refugees resulting from the Ogaden border war.
All these required a tremendous increase of foreign grants, loans, and other forms of aids.

Somalia continued to receive foreign grants in this period (1975-1979), most of the assistance being from Saudi Arabia and other Arab countries. As at December 1979, Somalia's long-term debt amounted to 4.6 billion Somali shillings (Knezevic, 41).

Banking System

The main features of the banking system of the Somali Democratic Republic were:
1. Designation of the Somali National Bank as the central bank of the country;

58

2. Creation of the Somali Commercial Bank and Somali Credit
and Savings Bank, which took over the commercial banking
activities in the country; and
3. Taking over of medium and long-term lending by the
Somali Development Bank, established in 1968.
Development of commercial banks was not significant and there
was not much effort to develop private savings. The Somali
Development Bank plays an important role in the
industrialization of the country by setting up and managing
industries and extending loans to other government agencies and
privately owned industries.

Audit Control

An important amendment was made in the laws to strengthen
post-audit of expenditures thereby reducing the requirement of
prior control on the legality of transactions by the Magistrate
of Accounts. This resulted from the fact that the expenditure of
substantial public funds could not be properly accounted for in
several former Ministries, including the former Prime Minister's
office and the Minister of Interior.
       A significant feature contained in this amendment was the
creation of a single unit for audit of public agencies, which was
an area previously outside financial control of the state (Legum,
B-175).

Finances of Public Agencies

The Ministry of Finance passed a law in 1973 on "Finances of
Public Enterprises and Agencies" in an effort to unify the system
of finance and accounting for public autonomous agencies and to
strengthen centralized control. This new law provides for an
integration of the finances of public agencies with the central
budget through a scheme of planned contributions by the
agencies to the central budget and vice versa.
       It is notable that after this law became effective, public
enterprises contributed much to budget stability, and the

government's share in the profit of public enterprises increased considerably (Knezevic, 15).

Personnel System

Until 1978 when the Somali government underwent some internal changes resulting from a reorganization of functions, the personnel system remained structurally unchanged from the previous system of government. The revision, which occurred in terms of personnel administration, was in terms of outlook and attitude.

As mentioned previously, the Somali Institute of Public Administration played a significant role in the administrative and structural changes in government. This was true of the personnel system only insofar as training was concerned in the area of Scientific Socialism. In a manual compiled by SIPA at the request of the government titled, "Duties and Responsibilities of Personnel Officers Working in Ministries and Agencies," one of the courses being offered to civil servants was "Attitudinal Changes Required of the Somali Civil Servants (Manual compiled by SIPA)."

Various measures were taken by the government to improve personnel administration and expand training and educational opportunities to increase the supply of personnel with requisite administrative and managerial skills and inspiration to achieve development goals. This was done by a revision of the Civil Service Law.

The Civil Service Law was revised to reflect the aims of revolution and principles of scientific socialism. The new law decentralized powers for disciplinary action and simplified procedures. The law contains provisions for elements of social justice and administrative efficiency of recruitment, promotion and disciplinary actions. The law also delegated personnel powers to the lower echelons of government and to the regional and district administrators and therefore, met in part the requirements of administrative decentralization for economic development.

All training of civil servants has been entrusted to the Somalia Institute of Public Administration Courses are included

for middle-management positions as well as for doctors, engineers, geologists, architects, lawyers, and chemists.
A pensions and gratuities law for civil servants was enacted in 1970. It entitled for the first time all Somali civil servants to the termination benefits. Terminal benefits were also extended to the employees of autonomous agencies in 1972.

Through a presidential circular in March 1972, temporary employees were absorbed into the permanent establishment of the ministries. Placement of the temporary staff was effected from their initial date of entry.

Since the civil servants are considered by the Supreme Revolutionary Council to be the "backbone of administration," a program of political orientation in the knowledge of scientific socialism for full political consciousness and commitment to economic progress was initiated. This helps the civil servant in understanding fully the meaning of the social philosophy and their role in the broad framework of the Republic.
Overall, the personnel system has been revised, not reconstructed with a major emphasis on the role of public administration in building a socialist system in the country.

Economic Development

From the beginning of the period of government by the Supreme Revolutionary Council in 1970 to the present, Somalia has witnessed some high achievements in the area of economic development. Some of the programs and steps undertaken by the government were bold and well-conceived. These include the

Agricultural Crash

Programs, the settlement schemes for the nomadic population the rapid increase in education, the construction of a large number of school buildings, the mass literacy campaign and introduction of Somali script, the disease eradication campaign of 1974, and the dramatic improvement in the Government's recurrent budgetary position (Kenzevic, 29). The capacity of the government to implement the projects successfully was much better compared to previous administrations.

In the area of agriculture, just at the time that production was beginning to show results, a disastrous drought hit the country in 1973 and lasted through 1974. Production in all agricultural sectors decreased affecting production of the manufacturing sector and transport.

In the area of fisheries, a Somali-Soviet Fishing Expedition started in 1972 and is at present still in force. In the area of water resources, a number of wells, basins were dug and equipment was purchased for the beginning of urban water supply schemes. In the area of mining, geological surveys in uranium, piezo-quartz, copper, manganese, lead, and zinc are still continuing.

One of the major concerns of the government was the development of industry and a number of large industrial enterprises were nationalized and new industries were established.

Outcome

The country's production has been growing at a modest but positive rate. Some important achievements have been made in development of the infrastructure (social and economic) industrial production, livestock development, fisheries, etc. A country using the best of its resources, in light of the many difficulties encountered, could only do all these.

Since statistical information is still at a minimum, it is not easy to make a full assessment of either total output or of the real growth of the Somali economy; however, for the first time in 1978, attempts were made to produce national income estimates, one by the Ministry of National Planning with the assistance of the United Nations and the other by the World Bank.

In concluding this study, the following chapter will look at developments within the past two years and the situation at present.

CHAPTER VII

CONCLUSION

As mentioned in the Introduction and repeated about this study, one of the limiting factors in the developmental history of Somalia has been the constant border conflicts with Ethiopia. The Ogaden border, which lies southeast of the Ethiopian highlands, has become the scene of numerous wars, the most recent in 1977-78 when Somali was defeated for lack of an available arms-supplier. As a result of this defeat, there was an influx of 1,200,000 refugees into Somali camps. This refugee population resulted in severe setbacks for the country in terms of military, political, diplomatic, and economic development (Europa Year Book, 1359).

Further Developments

Military

President Barre's "tough, well-trained" army said to be one of the best in the African Horn, was rippled in Ogaden in early 1978 because of a lack of military equipment. This led to dissatisfaction within the armed forces, which in turn resulted in a brief, disorganized, and ultimately unsuccessful coup against the president (Legum, B-373).

Political

Despite the natural unity of the Somalians, and the attempt by the President to crush the worst of tribalism, some Somalians feel that the President uses clan politics for his convenience in direct contravention of the basic principle in the operation of a Scientific Socialist government. Charges of nepotism and favoritism have been made. It is alleged that many administrative positions in the government have been filled by members of his own clan. In addition, the failure to acquire arms for the Somalian army has led to wide criticism of the handling of foreign affairs. Somalians are becoming, for the first time since the beginning of this administration, dissatisfied with the political prospects of the country (Legum, B-372).

Diplomatic and Foreign Relations

Relations with the U.S.S.R. were severed when, according to a "Newsweek" report in May of 1977, the Soviets and Somalia "did not see eye to eye on Ethiopia (Legum, B-372). However, in February of 1978, the Soviet Union put forward new proposals which included:

    a. The withdrawal of all regular Somali military units from the Ogaden;

    b. A promise by Somalia to respect Ethiopia's internationally recognized boundaries;

    c. A formal renunciation of Somalia's claims to Djibouti and Kenya's NFD;

    d. A regranting of Soviet rights to Somali naval facilities; and

    e. Somalia's participation in a political grouping with Ethiopia and South Yemen (Legum, B-374).

In return for acceptance of these proposals, Somalia would receive a promise of resumption of Soviet military and economic aid.

This time, President Barre, in his first conciliatory move, accepted the Soviet proposals stated above for consideration. In the months that ensued, however, the President found that his countrymen had many objections to the Soviet proposals. Consequently, he has not been able to convince his government to accept them (Legum, B-382).

Relations with the West, especially with the United States, have been clouded because of the West's failure to understand the true nature of the problems in the Horn of Africa. On one occasion, for example, an American newspaper branded Somalians as "terrorists," a charge which provoked an angry reply that "the righteous struggle of movements fighting oppression and colonialism was justified and could not be described as 'terrorism' (Legum, B-383).

The Somalians also claimed that if the United States had not previously promised them military aid, they would not have gone into Ogaden as unprepared as they obviously were. However, in March of 1978, after tempers had eased, President Carter promised to resume economic aid to Somalia in order to help renew its economic development programs (Legum, B-383).

Economic Development

In addition to the Ogaden war and other related factors mentioned above, the international monetary trade and energy crisis, plus a severe drought which hit the country during this period (1977-1980), slowed economic development. As a result of the drought, the five-year development plan, which included a large number of on-going projects, had to be stopped, inasmuch as the emphasis had been placed on agriculture and livestock.
The long-term objective of this program was to raise the standard of living of the people by providing opportunities for gainful employment, eradication of all forms of exploitation, and creation of a society based on the principles of social justice and individual freedom. The long-term strategy of economic development was oriented towards maximization of resource utilization, equitable distribution of the national product, decentralization of administration, social organization of production, better utilization of internal resources, and creation of a cooperative movement (Somalia: Economic Development, SOM/78/008). Obviously, because of the problems discussed above, the goals have not been realized.

Social Development

Perhaps the most remarkable success during the period was the "Mass Literacy Campaign" coupled with the introduction of the Somali script.
In education, there has been since 1969, an increase in the number of primary and secondary schools and the initiation of an adult education program for the nomads. Five new sections in post-secondary education have been started in the fields of medicine, veterinarian science, engineering, chemistry, and

geology.

Achievements were also made in the trade sector as internal distribution systems were expanded and improved in the fields of food production, construction materials, fuel, and the collection of hides and skins.

Better medical care has been achieved for the mass population by the creation of a basic health-care structure throughout the country. To attract tourist business, two excellent hotel facilities have been constructed in addition to three radio transmitters, and new airfields.

It is obvious that the numerous and rapid changes in administration in Somali history have left lasting effects on the country. It is a wonder that throughout these changes, a certain degree of integrity was maintained by the Somalians, an integrity stemming directly from their traditional unified heritage. The period of colonialism left continuing effects on the country, a fact made evident in a speech by President Barre to the nation, after the unsuccessful coup against him. In a radio broadcast, he stated that "colonialism, which has many faces, both old and new, all along wan t.ed to stir up chaos through its 'lackeys' (Legum, B-373).

Celebrating the ninth anniversary of Scientific Socialism, the President, in his speech to the nation, remarked:

> "It is necessary that all members of the society at large realize their responsibility towards the country, as well as their rights. It is as a result of this that the Central Committee decided and approved the making of a Constitution which will be promulgated during the coming year. In our opinion this will be a very important step for the democratic development which our country is seeking. Certainly, the Constitution will result in the establishment of a Parliament in which the various social strata will express their views about the policy and administration of the country (Legum, B-379)."

In January of 1979, the Somali Revolutionary Socialist Party Congress approved a draft Constitution which stipulates, among other things, that Somalia should pursue a policy of nonalignment; that a "People's Parliament" should be set up; and that the election of the President of the Republic should be by popular vote.

The new Constitution was implemented in September 1979 and elections were held in December 1979. As a result, the Somali government underwent internal changes resulting in a further reorganization of functions.

The following changes were made:

· The Bureaus of Economy and Finance were merged to become the Financial and Economic Bureau.

· The duties of the Defense and Security Bureaus were transferred to the Party Research Committee.

· The National Tourism Agency was upgraded to become the Ministry of Tourism (Legum, B-380).

Part II

One Man's Influence On Somalia:

The Life of Sheikh Al-Sharif Mahamud

Chapter VIII

The Making of a Man: Biographical Background

Sheikh Al-Sharif Mahamud was born in Ethiopia in 1895.
He was taller than the average Somali. He had a dark complexion
and spoke in a vibrant voice. His love for Allah, Somalia and
African people attracted many people from Somalia, Zanzibar,
Mombasa, Ethiopia, and specifically the Oromo and Eritrean
people to him. His family traces back to the "Ahlul-Bayt Tribe of
Saarrman" whose family came from Hijaz, Saudi Arabia. They
eventually made hijra (migration) to Persia (now known as Iran)
into the region of Jilan. They then made hijra to Benadir, Somali
to a small town of Saarrman close to Beydowa to spread the
Message of Allah to all of Africa from Beydowa.

Sheikh Al- Sharif Mahamud was in exile in Barawa
during the fascist Italian rule in Somalia and married into the
Baraweni community who were descendants of Hatim Taaee
from Saudi Arabia, and had seven children. Five of his children
were boys and two were girls. One was a Colonel of the Somali
Army and died in 1977 during the Somali Ogaden war with
Ethiopia. He believed and practiced the precepts that love could
foil hatred, and aggression could be won over by forgiveness. He
overcame the ignorance of the people with the knowledge of
Islam and Prophet Muhammad.

He was generous to his people and whenever he received
a gift he would give it to some needy person in Somalia, or
to the Mosques in Mombassa, Kenya, Zanzibar, Tanzania, or
Kampala. He could not turn away anyone in need and would
even prefer the needy over his own children and relatives.
He was a direct descendent of the Prophet Muhammad
through the Spiritual Leader of all the Saints of Islam,
Sheikh Abdul Qadir Al-Jilani whose lineage can be traced
back to Imam Hussein bin Ali, the grandson of the Prophet
Muhammad and to Imam 'Ali Ibn Abi Talib nephew of the
Prophet Muhammad and to Sayyida Fatimah Al Zahra, the
beloved daughter of our master and leader Prophet Muhammad.

Sheikh Al-Sharif Mahamud's father, Sheikh Abdur Rahman, was born in Ethiopia, and was a "Wali Allah", and the Khalifa of Tariqah Al-Qadiria, a Sufi spiritual order.

He was also a physicist and an astronomer who received his education in Baghdad, Iraq. His father, Sheikh Abdur Rahman (Rahimuhullah), was from "Ahlul-Bayt". He was a direct descendent of the Prophet Muhammad through the spiritual guide and leaders of all the saints of Islam, Sheikh Abdul Qadir Al-Jilani whose lineage goes back to Imam Hussein bin Ali, grandson of the Prophet Muhammad to Imam 'Ali Ibn Abi Talib nephew of the Prophet Muhammad and Sayyida Fatimah Al Zahra the beloved daughter of the Prophet Muhammad.
His mother was from the noble tribe of the "Ogaden" of Somali Ethiopia. She was believed to be a noble and religious Somali woman in Somali Ogaden in Ethiopia. She was a leader and community activist organizing and empowering all Muslim women in Ogaden and of the Darowood tribe decedent of Samaal who had once ruled Ethiopia, Sudan, and Egypt in the past. They were tall with a dark complexion. They were strong Black people who occupied the entire Horn of Africa from approximately 100 A. D. 90.

Chapter IX

The Importance of Education

Sheikh Al-Sharif Mahamud was a great scholar, Islamic theologian, mufti, and charismatic imam of Africa from Mogadishu, Somalia. He was an interpreter of the Qur'an, a scholar of Hadith, and an Islamic jurist. While in Qur'an school (Madrassa) in Ethiopia he was a leader. He started showing signs of excellence and was recognized by his teachers and the scholars in Ethiopia. When he was a small boy, his peers knew him as a pious child. He was also known for his education even before he had come of age.

As a child, Sheikh Al-Sharif Mahamud studied and memorized the Qur'an at the age of twelve. He travelled to the Holy City of Medina, Saudi Arabia, where he studied with scholars (Ulama Deen) of Medina and learned the Arabic language and literature. While there, he also received the "Ijaza" (permission) to preach. After the completion of his studies in Medina, he moved to Cairo, Egypt, to enroll at Al-Azhar University, the oldest university in the world.

He learned the fundamentals of Islamic theology and Islamic jurisprudence. In Cairo, he met Saad Zaaqlul the Egyptian leader who was fighting British colonialism and Jamal Al-Deen Al-Afghani, the scholar from Afghanistan. Sheikh Al-Sharif Mahamud was at the forefront of continuing the struggle to educate all Muslim Somali's and Africans with modern technology, and by educating them with science and math. Although, he was imprisoned in Barawa many times for disseminating literature against the west and after his release, was not allowed to travel for one year anywhere in the world, he continued doing lectures at the mosques on one nation, one Muslim and one *ummah.* He taught Qur'an, the Prophetic traditions, and sacred law, particularly to low–status individuals under western colonialism in the Swahili coast and gave a great amount of money to the Uwasia and the Ba-Alawi sufi orders in Barawe to establish Islamic Schools in Zanzjbar, Uganda, and Kenya.

Many scholars like Hadrami migrated from Barawa, Somalia to Zanzibar, Comoro, and Mozambique to establish Islamic studies. He helped by providing professional educators overseas from Saudi Arabia in the 1920's to Mogadishu, Merca, and Barawe, such as:
Teacher Al-Sharif Al Mushauaq from Al-Madina, Saudi Arabia.

- Teacher Abdullah Omar Bin Omar from Yemen.
- Teacher Omar Al-Shatter from Yemen.
- Teacher Muhammad Raza from Pakistan.
- Teacher Salem Abdullah Al Ajami from Iran.
- Teacher Muhammad Nasser from Iraq, to teach Somali people, Qur'an, Hadith and science.

He helped create Islamic schools in 1950 in Mogadishi, Somalia. He was the first to open schools with his own money in many cities in the Horn of Africa, like Al-Madrassa.

During his time in Ethiopia, with a long Islamic tradition of learning, Sheikh Al-Sharif Mahamud had the best instruction and social status in the society, full of respect for learning. He learned Qur'an, Hadith, physics and mathematics at an early age as well as Fiqh and the Arabic language. This happened to be possible because his uncles were scholars (Ulama) in Ethiopia. They influenced him through the teachings of Tafsir, Hadith, Sirah, Fiqh, Arabic language, mathematics, and physics.

He learned the Qur'an and Arabic language at an early age in Ethiopia. His relatives, particularly his uncles, were learned scholars ('Ulama) in Qur'an, Hadith, Shariah, Fiqh, physics, math, astronomy, and the Arabic language and were certified with Ijazas from Baghdad, Iraq. The environment of Islamic and secular scholarship served him to form and mold the character of a young boy who would go on to be one of Africa's and Islam's greatest imams and muftis.

Sheikh Al-Sharif Mahamud encouraged the learning of Arabic language in East African schools and that every leader should prepare to sacrifice and become an activist in Islam.

Sheikh Al-Sharif Mahamud with Al-Sharif Aydrus, founder of Al-Mahfal Al-Islam in Mogadishu, and Al Sheik Noor, founder of Eritrea Liberation Movement, organized the Horn of Africa Muslims Conference in Mogadishu, Somalia, which in turn organized the leaders of the Horn of Africa for *dawah*.
Sheikh Al-Sharif Mahamud was among the few leaders who had high concerns about teaching Arabic and Islamic education to all of Africa. He lectured in the Horn of Africa in the highest level of legitimate speaking tone for the concerns and aspirations of the entire African community in the Horn of Africa council of Government. Many Africans from the Horn of Africa respected the Sheikh, especially Oromos, for his honesty and love for the people.

He was especially close to the Oromo and Eritrean people for self-determination. He lectured in many masjids in the Horn of Africa and struggled hard to unite the leaders of all the tariqahs within the traditional Sufi order Muslim organizations and avoid to oppression of all other sects in all forms. His concerns were for all oppressed people in Africa whether Muslim or not, like other great African Muslim leaders. He helped create Islamic schools in 1950 in Mogadishi,

Somalia. He was the first to open schools with his own money in many cities in the Horn of Africa, like Al- Madrassa.

- Al-Madrassa Al-Falah
- Al-Madrassa Muhammad
- Al-Madrassa Al-IIuda
- Al-Madrassa Hafith Qur'an
- Al-Madrassa Al-Rabita Islamiya
- Al -Madrassa Al-Numudugia
- Al-Madrassa "ALLAH"

He lectured in Qur'an and Tafsir to Oromo communities in Ethiopia. Many times, he was invited to give lectures. They loved him as an African hero. He was preaching to the Horn of Africa families as one nation. He insisted that the Muslims of Africa should show love and respect for each other and that they should love Allah and Prophet Muhammad. He encouraged communities in Ethiopia to become self-sufficient and to get involved in social issues and to fight against colonialism and imperialism in

Somalia and all of Africa. They were instructed to be Hafiz of Qur'an and to work toward freedom and unity. Many of these scholars gave their lives for the freedom about which he preached. Al-Sharif reminded the people that the scholars had knowledge of Taqwa and Hadith and were heirs of the Prophets, and that they must respect the Ulama Al-D*een.* These were the descendants of Prophet Muhammad who had knowledge, taught the Qur'an and Sunnah, of which Muslims are benefiting from today.

Sheikh Al-Sharif Mahamud taught that when *iman (faith)* becomes less in Somalia, that every government would collapse, the people of Somalia would suffer and that it would lead to division and disaster. Those who believe in tribalism substitute their rituals for belief in God, as the only way to succeed in this life or they will surely perish. Sheikh Al-Sharif Mahamud founded Al-Rabita Al- Islamiya in Mogadishu, Somalia as the center of Da'wah to all of Africa.

Sheikh Al-Sharif Mahamud was the leader and Imam in Asmara, Eritrea and taught Qur'an and Tafsir Al-Sharif at the Mosque in Asmara. He had disciples scattered remotely in Oromo and Harary, Ethiopia and wanted to impart Islamic education through them by teaching them to start Arabic and Islamic schools throughout Africa and to liberate themselves from colonialism. Imam Al-Sharif provided resources and money for their activities and supplied books as donations. The leaders and scholars of these various communities were encouraged to participate in building moral and virtuous societies in Africa, and to promote family values in accordance with Islamic teachings. Emphasis was put on brotherhood, equality, justice, mercy, compassion, peace, and to foster unity in Africa for Muslims and non-Muslims.

The key issues were to fight ignorance, Africa's tribal systems, and immoral behavior in communities. The objective of the foundation, Al-Rabita *Islamiya* was for all of Africa to come together as Muslims into one Ummah. Sheikh Al-Sharif Mahamud lectured at Mosque Kampala, Uganda about his concern for Ugandans and specifically, Ugandan and Ethiopian Muslims. He criticized the atrocities of British colonialism in Africa, which made Africans less than animals. In his effort to combat ignorance, the Sheikh taught Tafsir, Qur'an and knowledge of Islam.

Through the education and lecturing on Qu'ran in Oromia, Eritrea, Uganda, and Kenya, he was invited to other parts of Africa to give lectures. They loved him for his Pan-Muslim views for Africa. He said "Africa's Muslims to unite is essential for your success! Africa needs freedom from the west." They were enjoying this beautiful, tall, black, charismatic leader from Somalia.

He gave many Gulf Arab students scholarships to attend Egyptian Universities and some of them attended the "Madrassa of Allah" in Mogadishu that he had founded in 1920. Some from Saudi Arabia, UAE, Oman, and Qatar attended his school and became leaders and ambassadors in their countries. Somalia and Oromia, historically one family, were mutual defenders with Gulf Arabs, aligned to defend the Qa'aba from before medieval times. Sheikh Al-Sharif Mahamud gave Muslim students scholarships from Zanzibar and Mombassa to attend the University of Al Azhar in Cairo, Egypt, and supported the struggle of Muslim communities of Uganda, Mombassa, Kenya, and the Muslim community in Zanzibar in Tanzania's resistance to European British colonialism, which was the main cause of much suffering and repression among the Muslim nations in the Horn of Africa. He also supported Muslim communities in South African and their leaders in their struggle against apartheid as well as supporting the Muslim communities in Mozambique.

Sheikh Al-Sharif Mahamud felt that all the subjects should be taught in Arabic, even science, math, philosophy and physics. The Sheikh had a strong love for students from Africa who loved Islamic education, such as the students from Gambia, Kenya, Uganda and Nigeria. With a deep love and connection to his beloved ancestor, he wrote many Khutbahs, praising the Prophet Muhammad, (peace and blessings of Allah be upon him), but none were published.

The Sheikh worked for the cause of Allahu ta 'ala, not expecting anything from the people he helped. He had high standards and work ethics, which allowed him to forge bonds of unity with the Arab world and was able to recruit the help of educators and specialists who came to Africa to teach in Somalia,

Eritrea, Mombassa, Zanzibar, Kampala and Uganda. Understanding the need for both a sound Islamic education and knowledge of modern technology, he was undoubtedly the reviver of traditional Islam in Africa, specifically the Horn of Africa through reform and struggles for the Muslim unity.

Sheikh Al-Sharif Mahamud also traveled to Mombasa, Kenya, Zanzibar, Tanzania, and many other cities in Somalia, where he noticed hunger, and widespread ignorance among the nomads, especially among the women and children in the north. Saddened by their plight, he invited nomads to learn modern technology and to improve skills in livestock management, fishing, and to adopt agriculture as a tool for survival. Sheikh Al-Sharif Mahamud encouraged kids and old students to go overseas to Egypt to get modern education in Arabic language and to become physicians.

Sheikh Al-Sharif Mahamud recruited many young Somali boys and girls to travel to Egypt to learn Islamic and modern sciences. He invited Somali parents to bring their students to the Masjid and to Duksy Qur'an school to gain Islamic education and to become Hafith of the Holy Qur'an. He distributed the Qur'an for free to all rural area kids and claimed that from now onwards, each one would receive free Qur'ans.

Sheikh Al-Sharif Mahamud offered to open schools with his money and to further help them in the future. He founded Al-Madrassa Al-Numudgia, an Elementary School, a High School of Allah, the Institute of Al-Azhar School of Nursing, and a School of Engineering. He motivated Northern Somalis to value knowledge in the medium of the Arabic language. He set up Islamic *madrassas* in 1920 and donated his money to build masjids in the Horn of Africa as well as to open clinics in Mogadishu. Schools opened by Sheikh Al- Sharif in Somali from 1920-1950 include:

- Institute of Islamic Studies
- Madrassa Alnumudugia
- Madrassa Al-Rabita
- Madrassa Al-Falah
- Islamic Library with international resources, books, science, periodical magazines and

newspapers from all over the Muslim world for free.

Sheikh Al-Sharif Mahamud emphasized in all his public lectures that Somalis should equip themselves with Islamic knowledge. His lectures, Friday khutbahs, and *marwass* were the glaring examples of bringing Somalia on the right track of not only religion but with a perspective of modern education.

Sheikh Al-Sharif Mahamud led Somali people towards global Muslim unity starting rightly from Somalia. He traveled to the north of the country to help open Islamic schools and to help improve living conditions through education. The sites he visited for this purpose include Zella, Booramo, Berber, Burao, Lasanod, Gerdo, Alula, Girban, El-dere, Huddur, and Beletweine. During the 1930's, he lectured at these locations on the importance of education and modern technology for Somalia and the rest of Africa.

Many in the Horn of Africa benefited from Sheik Al-Sharif's generosity. Generations of Somali and African youth received his support and he encouraged them to become scientists, leaders in the affairs of their communities, to spread the *deen* to African people, and to create an Islamic State. He obligated everyone to support the elderly, women, and children. Many of his students became great leaders, such as businessman, military chiefs, professors, and medical doctors.

The Sheikh was not a politician but rather hated politics. However, he loved the masjid, the Book of Allah, and Hadith, of which he read every day and followed practically for his entire life. This naturally led him to an open rejection of all the false and fake western political ideologies, such as, fascism, secularism, communism, and extreme capitalism.

In Somalia, a small portion of his clan of Ahlul Bayt lived in the town close to Beidowa called Al-Sarrman (the Jilani Communities). Thus, he had no affiliation with any tribe or political party whatsoever. He lived and died in neutrality in his approach towards the people of Somalia. Sheikh Al-Sharif Mahamud was a leader in Africa and the Arab Gulf by helping everybody flee the persecution of British Colonialism in the Arab Gulf, Kenya, Uganda, and Tanganyika. He helped all those he encountered morally, financially, and spiritually. He, along with Arab groups, helped in spreading the *deen* of Allah deep into Africa through opening madrassas (schools).

He worked with Arab Muslim leaders together to unite all Muslims in the world. He lectured throughout the Horn of Africa and helped in building Mosques in Zanzibar and Mombasa, and taught Islamic education to the followers of Uwesia from Barawe who originated from Somalia in Zanzibar, and Mombassa. They wanted to unite with Al-Rabita Al- Islamiya in Mogadishu, Somalia.

They were pro-Muslim unity and were relatives of Somalia Barawa and originated from Arab Omani, and Yemen Barawe. They united with Muslim Brotherhood communities in East Africa, the leadership movement Khalifa al-Qadiryya of Balawi Somali Hadrami and the Khalifa of Uweisiya from Barawe, Somalia.

Sheikh Al-Sharif Mahamud helped Zanzibar, Mombassa, and Kampla with instructors from Al-Azhar University in Egypt to teach Qur'an, Hadith, and Arabic language for free.

In Mogadishu, the Somali Benadir respected scholars (Ulama) of the *deen*, Qadis (Judge) of the Somali Benadir, and people from the coast of Africa. They maintained open communication between them.

Many of them worked to teach Islam and to educate the masses of the Islamic forces in Mogadishu. It was a history of sufism and Islamic activism, which was established by the Khalifa in Barawa. They were organizing and teaching knowledge of the Prophet Muhammad.

Mogadishu and Barawe, Somalia were the cities of peace and were the Centers of the Khalifa of the Al-Qadiryya Sufi order. According to Sheikh Al-Sharif Mahamud, Mogadishu was the city of peace and was the center of the Khalifa of Al-Qadiryya Sufi order. It was also the center of leadership for the Muslims' world communities and a city of multiculturalism.

He advocated Islam as a solution to the ills of African people and the entire Islamic worlds. He was against clanship, secularism, and communism that had befallen and divided the Somali and African Muslim communities.

Sheikh Al-Sharif Mahamud dedicated his entire life to serving African people, the poor, the illiterate laborers, and poor farmers in the villages that were exploited by Italian fascists. Sheikh Al-Sharif Mahamud was among the first who stood to defend African people and protest slavery and injustice in East Africa. He wrote letters to the USSR and China requesting their support for Africa's struggle for freedom and independence. Sheikh Al-Sharif Mahamud preached dignity for African people. He preached dignity (Karamah) to all Somalis and Africans in the mosque of "Hamarwean" and in the Horn of Africa and encouraged them to unite all African Muslims.

He was inseparably linked with the hopes and aspirations of the Muslims in Africa, the joys and sorrows, the trials and triumphs.

Chapter X

Importance of Islam and Unification

During the Siad Barre regime in 1969, Sheikh Al-Sharif Mahamud protested against the military's ideology who took over the Somali Government by force, instead wanting an Islamic Government in the entire Horn of Africa ruled by the Sharia.

He deeply worried about Africa and the violation of the Sharia and the neglect of the Qur'an and sunnah of the Prophet Muhammad in the Horn of Africa.

Sheikh Sharif Mahamud said all must study the life of the Holy Prophet Muhammed before getting involved in tribal leadership. As Muslims, all Somali people must love the Prophet Mohammed as the best example to follow. His message of Islam, his teachings and his Sunnah are valid to all Somalis. While some Somalis believed that the tribal chiefs would bring prosperity to Somalia, Sheikh Sharif strongly objected. He said that the wealth and the blessings for the Somali people were the gifts of the Qur'an and Sunnah, that Allah had given us the entire Prophet Muhammad, and he was the perfect example of how to apply our religion in every aspect of our lives including schools, universities and in government affairs.

Sheikh Al-Sharif Mahamud said every Somali must submit to the revelation of Allah. No one was free to accept pro-western ideology in the Horn of Africa, as Muslims were prohibited by Allah to accept their way of life. Every aspect of their lives had to be governed by the Qur'an and Sunnah. Any act of worship was to be done for the sake of Allah and not for tribe, clan, socialism, or communism.

Sheikh Al-Sharif was also a teacher of faith to the nomads in rural areas. He said, "Islam first crossed in Abyssinia and spread over to the Horn of Africa even before going to Medina, a matter of profound significance to us as African nations. We are the eye of Islam all over the world. The wisdom, which we are yet to be proud of as a leader of the Horn of African, unfolds in the future."

Sheikh Al-Sharif Mahamud said that Islam is in the blood of the people of Somalia and that nobody in the world could make them different. Throughout history, Somalia produced the best *Ulama al Deen* of the world in Mogadishu, who traveled to West Africa and Asia to teach Islam. Al-Sharif taught Somalis that nothing was wrong with being African, despite their having this problem of identity for over six hundred years. "Understand who you are and defend the Book of Allah, and believe that the unity of Muslims of Africa is essential to unify Muslims of the world."

Many leaders and scholars of Islam respected Sheikh Al-Sharif Mahamud, such as Sheikh Hajji Sufi, a scholar from Ogaden of Ethiopia who was a very close friend to him for many years. During Siad Barre's regime, he suggested to President Barre to honor Sheikh Al-Sharif Mahamud by establishing an Africa Islamic University in his name, but Barre rejected this idea. Many dignitaries from the Horn of Africa and Arab nations respected him and often visited him, such as President Aden Abdullah Othman, President Hajji Muhammad Hussein, General Dawood of the Somali Army, Dr. Abdi Rasheed Ali Shermarke, Ottoman Sabee of the Eritrea Liberation Movement, Muhammad Aden of Eritrea's Parliament, Sayeed Kassim Al-Mazru from Kenya, and even Michael Mariamo, the Christian leader from north Somaliland. In fact, when he traveled overseas to Saudi Arabia and Sudan, King Faisal gave him a Mercedes. He donated it to a mosque and never used it for himself.

The Sheikh succeeded in his objectives by uniting the Sufi Qadirya order from the Horn of Africa and united it with the Qadiriya in Mombasa, Zanzibar and Mozambique toward African unity. He preserved the revival of the Islamic ways of life through opposing colonialism, and imperialism and defending Muslims Dignity (Karama) and the oppressed African people in the continent. The Somali Benadir were close to the coast of Swahili in Mombassa and Zanzibar and were the families of Rear Hammer from Barawe, such as Hatimi and Al-Sharif Ba Alawi. The majority of these families were against the British and were pro-Muslim brotherhood. Al-Rabita Al-Islamiya were united all Tariqa Oredr such as Sufi Qadiriya,Amadiya,Rufaiya, and their center was in Barawe, Somalia. Al-Rabita Al-Islamiya led all

Muslim organization in the coast of Swahili to unite all of Africa under the Al-Rabita-Al-Islamiya Muslim brotherhood. They were communicating with Muslim all over Africa and the west was mechanically interested in dividing Africa and Arab and Muslim movements in Mombasa and Zanzibar – specifically Afro Arab in Hrare in Ethiopia, and Eritrea.the Somali Muslim Brotherhood of the Al-Rabita Al-Islamiya under Sheikh Al-Sharif Mahamud was active in unification all muslim all over the world.

Sheikh Al-Sharif Mahamud founded the "Ahlul-Bayt" in Beydowa movement to unite all Ahlul-Bayt in all Africa, in 1920 and to unite all Muslims in the Horn of Africa. The movement was successful in the beginning until west and Ethiopia attack the movement .Al Sheik Al-Sharif Mahamud founded anther movement to west and Ethiopia involvement in Somalia under the Al-Rabita Al-Islamiya's leadership. He created this movement to help educate people in the Horn of Africa and to unite all Africans under Al-Rabita Al-Islamiya in Mogadishu, Somalia. The communities from Rear Hammer supporter of Ahlul-Bayt loved Sheikh Al-Sharif and the motherland and were devoted Muslims who became members of Al-Rabita Al-Islamya. Many were killed in Mogadishu for the sake of Islamic unity and Somali unity in the Horn of Africa.

In 1954, the Egyptian representative to the U. N., Ambassador Muhammad Kamal Al–Din Saleh, worked with Sheikh Al-Sharif Mahamud to unite all Somalis under one Muslim shelter. The Ambassador was a victim of the German, Italian, English, and the French. The United States allied with Ethiopia, to divide Somali into many parts. Further, they had a future plan for Ethiopian Christians to rule the divided land. Their interest was to divide Somalia into many clans and tribal systems.

He organized meetings to warn Somali people about the dangerous tribal fascists in Somalia and secretly, with leaders from Rahaweyn (Digil-Mirifle). The leaders from Tariqa in Beidowa and the majority of the leaders who attended the meeting where pro-Sheikh Al-Sharif Mahamud and pro-Muslim. In attendance were leaders such as, Omar Bana Funzi and Hajji Mohamed Hussein, Faqii Otman, Deira Hajji Deiira, Hajji Abass, Hajji Nur Al Brawi, Hajji Schafi and the Ambassadors to Egypt and Pakistan, whom were supporting unity of Muslims for the sake of Islam. The two Ambassadors warned Somali people against tribal fascism and westernization and said that western governments had plans to make Somalis into slaves for Ethiopia and to further divide them into many clans and tribes. Those who heard the warnings were very angry against the West and hated the Italians, English, French, Ethiopians, and Germans. The West decided to divide Somali Benadir along with the rest of Somalia, but the leader of Somali Benadir was against western imperialism. He wrote to many Muslim leaders all over the world to support Somalia's struggle for unity in Somalia.

Sheikh Al-Sharif Mahamud always resisted against the Anglo-Italo-Ethiopian boundaries and invited all leaders from north Somaliland, and Djibouti, Somali N. F. D to come to Mogadishu, Somali Benadir and to hold demonstration against the west by protesting for the elimination of these artificial boundaries, which were created by western fascist powers. Sheikh Al-Sharif Mahamud helped to organize the communities of Khalifa of Qadiriya, the follower of Sheikh Uways Al-Barawi from Barawa to Zanzibar, Mozambique and Ba-Alawi Al-Qadiryya to unite with Al-Rabita Al-*Islamiya*, from Mogadishu. This unification was formed to bring all Muslim groups into one Muslim organization for defending Islam and African people. Most Muslim leaders of Africa were close to the

Khalifa of Al-Qadiriyya in Barawa. They led the movement of Qadiriya from Mozambique, Congo, and Tanganyika to India. Their mission was for one Ummah seeking peace, freedom, and justice for all, and to work for education to teach African people Islam and Arabic language.
Sheikh Al-Sharif Mahamud helped to unite the east African Muslim communities in the 1920's and 1930's such as, Ethiopia's Sidamo, Oromo, Afar, Somalis from Al-Rabita Al-*Islamiya*, Muslim Brotherhood movement league, and Sheikh Abraham Sultan from Eritrea.

All of these people were committed to defend the values of the Qur'an and Sunnah for the sake of Allah. All Sufi Orders were united under one Khalifa. The various movements and organizations loved the Prophet Muhammad and defended him. The scholars of Qadiryya in Barawe, and the son of Sheikh

Uweis Qadiriya, Sheikh Saqwa-Deen organized a huge movement from Rahawan, Digil, Jiidu, Tunni, Garre, Ajuraan and Debarre to support Sheikh Al-Sharif Mahamaud Al-Saarmaan to be Obeyed and loyal to him and to protect him while he was lecturing in Somali Ogaden in Ethiopia. Sheikh Saqwa-Deen also loved Sheikh Al-Sharif Mahamud and was very serious in the unity of Muslims in Africa. He was very active in many organizations in Somalia and was the leader of Al-Qadiriya from Barawe, Lamu, Mombassa, Comoro, Mozambique and South Africa.

Sheikh Al-Sharif Mahamud visited presidents and kings and sheiks in the Arab Gulf in 1953, such as Jamal Abdunassiir, King Hussein of Jordan, King Hassan of Morocco, King Al Sud of Saudi Arabia, president of Burkiba of Tunisia, the president of Lebanon, and the president of Pakistan. He urged Arab and Muslim leaders to help him in uniting Somalia and to make it independent from Ethiopia.

He also encouraged them to invest in African Islamic education and to open madrassas in Africa. Sheikh Al-Sharif Mahamud believed that African and Arab unity was essential for world peace. He sent delegations to spread Islam around the world. He suggested investment ideas to Arab presidents for the sake of Africa's growth and development in modern technology and Islamic propagation. He was always proud to be Somali and African. He always wanted Somalia to be the leader of the Islamic world and to lead in African affairs. By gaining education in Islam, science, math, and modern technology, his vision, he believed, would be possible. He said in his address to all Somalis at the Mosque of Marwass, "Our goal as Horn of Africa communities is to work together for the Islamization of all of Africa. The Somali and Arab communities must unite under the Book of Allah and the Sunnah".

He rhetorically asked, "Do we want the Somali people to live as nomads, uneducated all our lives, and hate ourselves and fight among ourselves for clan power, going around-in circles like Somalis killing Somalis, and clan killing clan for almost six hundred years?" The best celebration of his life was in 1940-1941. For the first time in forty years, the Somali Ogaden united with Southern and Northern Somaliland. He was very happy and he celebrated with other Muslims from Uganda, Sudan, Eritrea, Ethiopia, and Saudi Arabia. He said that the Horn of Africa will become united as a nation one day, and will become an Islamic States in the future.

His goal was to unify the entire Muslim world and specifically the Horn of Africa. He organized Al-Rabita Al-*Islamiya*, the Muslim Brotherhood Movement league in Mogadishu, Somalia in 1921. The people of the Horn Africa are historically from the Qahtanis family who are originally from Yemen. Somalia has always had an identity problem and has struggled for years with their identity under the banner of African Muslim Unity between Sudan, Ethiopia, Somalia, Uganda, Kenya, Tanzania, Comoro, and Mozambique.

Scholars of Horn of Africa where impressed with Imam Sheikh Al-Sharif Mahamud, the leader of Al-Rabita Al108 Islamiya in Mogadishu,Somalia was elected as the leader from the Horn of Africa in order to unite all Muslims unto one Ummah. The objective of Al-Rabita Al-Islamiya was to build schools and Mosques across the Horn of Africa.

Al-Rabita Al-Islamiya had united all Muslim organizations in the Horn of Africa, such as Khalifa of Al-Qadiriya of Harar in Ethiopia, Khalifa of Al-Qadiriya of Eritrea, Khalifa of Ba-Alawi Al-Qadiriya Al-Barawi, Khalifa of Shaekh Uwyes Al-Barawi from Barawa, Sheikh Hajji Rufaii Al-Barawi from Swahili the coast in Mombassa, Khalifa Sheikh Saeed Ahmed Ba-Alawi from Comoro, Khalifa Sheikh Mohamed from Tanzania, and Sheikh Hajji Sufi Al-Barawi from Mozambique.

He helped to unite all Somali leaders from the north to the south and aided all Muslim organizations to support one another, specifically the community of Merca and Barawa-Sufi order. The Somali Hadrami were the backbone of the Somali people who had always believed that they were Somali and African with a proud African heritage. Most of them were educated businessmen, doctors, pharmacists, government administrators, and scholars Hadrami. Many of them were Ulama and were leaders in the communities who were working for Somali unity and African unity, but the allied conspiracy between Ethiopia and the West was successful in driving them from the Horn of Africa back to the Arabian Peninsula.

The purpose of Al-Rabita Al-Islamiya was to unite all Muslims around the world, and to unite Somali Communities and Muslims from all over the Horn of Africa as one nation, and to replace tribalism with the book of Allah and the sunnah of the Prophet Muhammad and to work for Somalia's independence, and to free all of Africa from colonialism.

Chapter XI

Political Landscape

In 1921 Sheikh Al-Sharif Mahamud was selected as Chief of the Confederacy of the Horn of Africa Muslim Consultation by the Al Shura Africa society from the Horn of Africa communities in Mogadishu and was elected as Mufti and leader of the Horn of Africa.

Though he didn't want to become a leader of Africa, he took up the challenge and fulfilled his obligation and was greatly appreciated for his leadership. His role model was Prophet Muhammad for spreading the Deen of Allah to all of Africa. He lectured in several cities and states in Africa, based on the Holy Qur'an and the authentic sunnah. His role as the father of Somalia's freedom from colonialism was ended, diminished, and unrecognized by the Siad Barre Government, which labeled him as an enemy of the October Revolution. "Al –Sarrman Ahlul Bayt" and their Affiliation of Rahawyen from Digil and Mirefly from Somali Benadir were suspected to be pro-Sheikh Al-Sharif Muhammad and against Siad Barre's regime. Barre declared that his struggle was an open challenge to the right of the Barre regime and considered him an open anti-state element.

The Emperor, Haile Selassie of Ethiopia, was opposed to Sheikh Al-Sharif Mahamud for establishing Al-Rabita Al-Islamiya for the Horn of Africa Muslim unity, and pro-Ethiopia and westerners were strong at that time in Mogadishu. All were propagating against Rear-Hammer unity under the leadership of Sheikh Al-Sharif Mahamud. As a child, Haile Selassie had lived in Harar, Somali Ogaden and hate Islam and Arabic Language and he fear Ahlul-Bayt communities.He organized tribali system in Somali ogaden to attack Arab Communities in Harare who were pro Rear Hammer pro Islam unity in Somali Benadir. He spoke Somali language fluently and knew Somali culture, but he was against Muslim unity in Horn of Africa. However, Emperor Haile Selassie was cleverly close to the leaders of Somali in Muduq and Somali Djibouti, Somali Benadir ,and Somali Ogaden and used them to his benefit - to gain control over all of Somalia. Consequently, this led him to create hurdles in Somali Muslim unity in the Horn of Africa.

Emperor Selassie paid the same Somali clan leaders in Somali Benadir in the shape of monthly salaries and created a very powerful Pro-Ethiopian bloc in Mogadishu. In the 1950s, the Somali clan leaders were against Sheikh Al-Sharif Mahamud and against an Islamic State in Somali Benadir. Hail Selassie unified pro-west Somalis, most of whom were from the Muduq area, and pro-Ethiopian tribal leaders from Somalia who encouraged the creation of a political party pro west in all of Somalia.

The pro-west Muduq in Somali Benadir were propagated in Jannaale on the Shabeele River and Jubba near Chismayo. Their objective was to assist in the transcription of Somali language to Ethiopian or Latin script and to create a church in the region which also included Barawe, Merca, and Mogadishu. They were recruiting Muslims from Somali Benadir to convert them to Christianity and to turn them against Sheikh Al-Sharif Mahamaud's idea of an Islamic State. This fact helps to provide the norm for cementing Islamic influence in most parts of Africa. Yet, a simple glance at any map of Africa will show the ugly face of tribalism as a new form of decision making by chiefs of clans and used as a fascist system to maintain power. These chiefs humiliated Muslim communities through intimidation and they fought Islam and Arabic language in Somalia with their political clans. In doing so, they aided the fascist Italian and Roman Catholic.Clan system in Somalia was created by the CIA of United States, Italy, France, Britain, and Christian Ethiopia's power structure. The country of Somalia was thus divided into its five parts by western intervention. It might never be united as Sheikh Al-Sharif Mahamud wanted.

Sheikh Al-Sharif Mahamud and all the leaders of Arab communities in Somali Benadir, who were pro-Muslim in Somalia and pro-unity with other Muslims in the Horn of Africa, were Arabs from Hdraamowt of Yemen , who lived in Mogadishu, Merca, Barawe thousands years ago, and Somalia. By the grace of Allah, their evil desires could not reach him, but in 1954 they killed the Egyptian representative, U. N. Ambassador Mohammad Kamal Al-Deen Saleh, who was working for unity in Somalia and unity of Muslims of the Horn of Africa with Sheikh Al-Sharif Mahamud. This unity would have extended from the Somali Benadir Rear Hammer to the Muslims in Mombasa, Kenya, Arab communities in Uganda, Zanzibar, Tanzania and Muslims from Ethiopia.

He was in correspondence with leaders and Imams of Ahlul Beyt from Balawi from Mombassa, Kenya,Zanzibar.Tanzania, who wanted to unify Muslims communities in Somali Benadir. Many Muslims in Zanzibar were close to Barawe communities and were relatives, such as Afro Barawe Hatimi in Mombassa, Afro Shiraz in Zanzibar, Tanzania, Afro Arab in Kampala,Uganda, Afro Somali in Khartoum,Sudan, and Afro Bajuni in Nairobi,Kenya. The same was true for Eritrea in Ethiopea, as many were Afro Somali who lived in the coast of Africa were relative to Hatimi of Somali Benadir and their relatives were close to Barawe, Somalia. These groups were pro-Islam, pro Al-Rabita Al- Islamiya and supported the unification of all Muslim communities. The Somali Harare and the Oromo, Eritreans were pro-Muslim unity too, but the United States, British, French, German and Catholic Crusaders were very strong against Muslim unity between African and Arab states.

Furthermore, they supported the division of Muslim organizations to generate confusion, assisting in the goal of killing the movement to make the Muslims of Kenya hate the Muslims of Somali and Zanzibar, as well as the renowned Muslim leaders in the Horn of Africa. This hatred also helped to fuel a shift in control of Somali Benadir, placing it under Christian leadership and eliminating Islamic and Arab Sufi movements in all of Africa.

In 1945, pro-west and pro-Ethiopian movements were created in Mogadishu. Tribal fascist also supported strong movements of pro-tribal fascism in Somali Benadir and in the Horn of Africa. They further supported pro-western movements by infiltrating Arab Muslim movements and by controlling all political organizations in the Horn of Africa. Sheikh Al-Sharif dedicated his life to working for the development of an Islamic State in the Horn of Africa and for the eradication of imperialism in all of Africa.

The Egyptian representative of the U. N. in Mogadishu in 1954, Ambassador Muhammad Kamal Al–Deen Saleh, worked very hard with Al-Sharif Mahamud to unite all of Somali and the Horn of Africa Muslims, holding the five Somali stars geographic location. In collaboration with other Muslims in Africa, he was committed to the development of an Islamic State in Somalia, but unfortunately, he was hated by pro-western Somalis, and was killed in Mogadishu under a European conspiracy. The Americans, Italians, British, Germans, and Ethiopians were united for the purpose of breaking up the Muslim movement from "Ahlul-Bayt," descendent of the Prophet Muhammed , who tried to unite all the Muslims in Africa by organizing Muslim Brotherhood unity in Mogadishu, Sudan, Ethiopia, Eritrea, Kenya, Tanzania, Mozambique, Congo, Gambia, and Nigeria. Ambassador Saleh worked with Al-Sharif Mahamud to unite all of Somalia. They were planning with SYL to move forward with leading Somalia into an Islamic State. The Germans, Italians, English, French and Ethiopians wanted Sheikh Al-Sharif Mahamud killed. Those who were pro-clan and pro-West were not educated and were unaware of the politics in the Horn of Africa. They were paid a lot of money to work with the Italians, Ethiopians and Roman Catholics to create a strong pro-West movement.

The pro-West of 1946 were stronger than the Muslim brotherhood. They fought and killed for the sake of money, tribal honor and tribal approval. They would never be arrested or killed by other tribes because their own tribes would protect them. These Muduqs did not care for the Muslims from Rear Hammer. A Muduq didn't care if this was Jahiliya, which was strong in Somalia until Sheikh Al-Sharif Mahamud intervened and fought against this behavior by lecturing at Masjid Hamerwyen. For years, he helped Arabs and Ahlul-Bayt who lived in Somali to evade murder, as he believed Somalis and Arabs to be of one family and one nation with one religion.

Sheikh Al-Sharif Mahamud and many Rear Hammer demonstrated by thousands in Mogadishu,Barawe,Merca against tribal fascism and pro-Islam unity and pro-Islamic education. He was a leader of Rear Hammer in Somali Benadir, but Ethiopian and European opponents wanted Somali Benadir to remain backwards and weakened by tribalism for many years. However, most of the shuyukh and scholars in Somali Benadir under his leadership fought against tribalism in all of Somalia and most Rear Hammer leaders self-identified as Somali and African, not tribally, as it was shameful in the1920s in Mogadishu to associate someone or oneself with tribal affiliations. Tribalism was considered to be a Backward, uncivilized , practice of the uneducated and was associated with opportunists and beggars who were unwilling to work in Mogadishu. Tribal leaders who were dependent on their tribe for support, feared other tribes and would therefore be against a larger Muslim identity. Sheikh Sharif Mahamud believed tribalism was a form of fascism in Africa and said "free yourselves from tribalism of Shaytan," seeing tribalism and clannishness as false forms of worship. Tribal fascism was a form of social security in Somali society, which harmed no one's health, but spelled disaster for unity of future generations. The fascist system created by the Germans, English, Italians, French, Americans, and Ethiopian Christian agencies were the wrong systems for the Somali people.

He said it is very important to know our nation, our culture and our identity as Somalis and Africans. The Ethiopian, British, and Italian governments wanted to eliminate Sheikh Al-Sharif Mahamud, but Somali leaders from communities in Mogadishu and leaders of Somali Benadir protected Sheikh Al-Sharif Mahamud from 1920-1960.

He said the West hatcd Somalia and would divide it into many parts and would scatter its people around the world. The Somali resources would be exploited by the Italians and the Somali people would be converted to Christianity and become part of Christian Ethiopia.

The West influenced Somali's trial leaders to create a clan system to engage against each other and to kill one another for the benefit of Ethiopia and the West. They wanted Al-Sharif to be assassinated because he was considered to be an enemy to such a plan. Ethiopia mistakenly thought he wanted to become a ruler of Somalia and all of Africa.

In 1960, the majority of Somali Benadir Rear Hammers were depressed the lost their Identity because of tribal become strong and the system of decision making in 1960 same of Rar

Hammer who were member of S.Y.L the supported SYL in their struggle against colnialism and they fought for Somali unity. And Somali Benadir and North Somaliland united in 1960 to become the Somali Republic, but Ethiopia and the West were not happy with Somali unification. The Rear Hammer under the leadership of Deira Haji Deira and Omar Bana Funzi pro Somali and Muslim unity were help elected President Aden Abdulla to fulfill the dream of Al-Sheikh Al-Sharif Mahamud, which was a pan-Somali Muslim union that would become the center of the Muslim world. The first president was elected by a majority vote of Rear Hammer in S.Y.L, which humiliated Ethiopia and the West.

He emerged as a strong leader in the Horn of Africa and was pro-Arab and Islam able to unite all Somalia and to empower all of Africa, but the Christian Ethiopia Government were Threatening and invade Somali Republic and West, specifically Britain, CIA U.S.A, Germany, and France, tried to overthrow him militarily. After six years, they replaced him with President Abdul Rashid. Western powers were interested in African resources, thus, they created the Organization for African Unity in Addis Ababa to avoid Muslim Brotherhood of African unity from Mogadishu Somalia and the founder was Al-Sheikh Al-Sharif Mahamud, as the center of all African affairs in Somalia . This was done to place Africa's international affairs under the leadership of the Amhara Christians in Ethiopia and out of the hands of Muslims in Somalia Benadir .General Dawood chief staff of Somaly Army was student of Al-Sheikh Al-Sharif Mahamud with Haji Mohamed Hussain and Omar Bana Funzi and close friend of President of Gamal Abdel Nasser of Egypt when he recruited many officials from Harare and Eritrea and Rear Hammer to become the leader of Somali Army and when he became the Chief of Staff for the Somali Army, the West and Ethiopia felt threatened by him, as he was a of Sheikh Al- Sharif Mahamud. He died mysteriously with of a strange sickness.

Ethiopian Christians controlled the Somali Ogaden by the support of Roman Catholics and the West. They killed many Somali from Ahlul-Bayt and Arab Hadrami from Yemen and many Arab Bani-Hashim who lived in Somali Ogaden and who were descendants of Prophet Muhammad. The Ethiopian Emperor was pro-Roman Catholic and influenced the indigenous Africans to attack Arab Africans in Somali Ogaden, and Arab in Mombassa, Kenya, and Zanzibar in Tanzania and Mogadishu, Merca, Barawe in Somalia. Sheik Al-Sharif Mahamud protected them and created the Muslim African movement league in the Horn of Africa to fight the Ethiopian treat in Somalia.When the north of Somalia suffered from starvation, disease, lack of education, and lack of healthcare. During this time, those who were pro-Ethiopians wanted to unite north Somalia with Ethiopia. Sheikh Al-Sharif Mahamud and Rer Hammer of Somali Bendir organize a big movement from all of Horn of Africa to supported North of Somali and all Muslims in the Horn of Africa where acted as one Muslim families in this Issue ad united to confront these problem by Fundraising.

In Mogadishu, at Masjiid Marwaas, Sheikh Al-Sharif Mahamud said that the leader of the Religious Sufi orders played a significant role in the movement of anti-colonialism and anti-fascism in the Horn of Africa and particularly in Somalia. According to Sheikh Al-Sharif Mahamud the Somali Rear Hammer originated from Qahtani and Himyar of Yemen, migrated and established them in the Horn of Africa, and then lived in Mogadishu for many years. The pre-Islamic Rear Hammer arrived in Somalia from Yemen after a civil war. They suffered defeat and migrated to Mogadishu to establish Himyar of the Yemen dynasty and were Arab descendants of Hadrami living in Mogadishu and Barawa.

These Arab communities in the Horn of Africa later supported the Al-Rabita Al-*Islamiya* Muslim Brotherhood movement league. The Somali Benadir Rear hammer fought against the Christian Ethiopians, Italian fascism, and Britain for many years. They fought bravely for Somali unity (Pan-Somalism), for African Muslim unity, and for independence and freedom from the Italian fascists at great personal costs. Sheikh Al-Sharif Mahamud said that there were many Rear Hammer members jailed during Italian colonialism and beaten in Merca, Barawa and Mogadishu. Sheikh Al-Sharif said the Italians tortured many Rear Hammer from Somali Benadir communities from Mogadishu. This caused too many Rear Hammer from

Somali communities of Hatimi and Banihashim to flee and emigrate to Mombassa.Kenya,Kampala. Uganda, and Zanzibar.Tanzania as refugees, fleeing persecution from Italian fascism in Mogadishu and Ethiopian Christian persecution in Somali Ogaden. Sheikh Al-Sharif Mahamud, Sheikh Noor from Eritrea, and Sheikh Abdurahman from Ethiopia's Oromo tribe came together in Mogadishu to mobilize the masses of Rear Hammer and to demonstrate against Italian fascism.

Sheikh Al-Sharif Muhammad gave lectures and *khutbahs* at the mosque in Merca in order to unify all Muslim organizations in their fight against Italy and the West. Sheikh Al-Sharif said the people of Rear Hammer always considered themselves as Muslim, Somali, and African. They were intermingled with indigenous of African for thousands of years, from Ethiopia, Kenya, Tanzania, and Mozambique.

They came from Hijaz, Saudi Arabia and were spreading Islam to the many parts of Africa. They were founders of Pan-Muslim brotherhood from Mogadishu-Somalia with a Muslim movement league to unite Africa. They fought for many years against Roman Christian and Ethiopian expansion in Somalia and against Portugal colonialism in the Horn of Africa.

Chapter XII

The Passing of a Legend

Sheikh Al-Sharif Mahamud became ill in his ninety-eighth year in 1992. He died in Cairo, Egypt. He had been offered treatment in a Pakistani hospital, however he refused. He wanted to die in Cairo, Egypt and was buried with Ahl-Al-beit from Sudan in Egypt and from there he returned to his Lord with his face directed towards the Qa'aba, the sacred house of Allah (SWT). Egypt was a second home for him where he had grown up as a child and spent his adult life with Ahl-Al-beit. May Allah (SWT) forgive his sins and veil his faults and accept him with honor and a beautiful covering and make him dwell in the highest place.

BIBLIOGRAPHY

BOOKS

Asad, Muhumad. The Principle of State and Government in
    Islam. California: Berkeley University Press, 1961.

Bayn, E. A. Somalia Poliotics and Government. New York:
    University Field Staff, 1965.

Castagno, Margaret. Historical Dictionary of Somalia.
    Metuchen, New Jersey: Legrecrow Press, 1975.

Finkelstein, Lawrence C. Somaliland Under Italian
    Administration: A Case Study in U.N. Trusteeship.
    New York: Woodrow Wilson Foundat~on, *1955.*

Hess, Robert L. Italian Colonialism In Somalia. Chicago:
    University Press, 1966.

Karp, Mark. The Economics of Trusteeship in Somalia.
    Boston: University Press, 1960.

Lewis, I.M. A Pastoral Democracy: Traditional Somali
    Society. London: Oxford Un~versity Press, 1961.

Lewis, I.M. People of the Horn of Africa. London:
    African Institute, 1965.

Lewis, I.M. The Modern History of Somaliland: From
    Nation to State. New York: Praeger Publishers, 1965.

Noor, Muhammad Haji. The Legal System of the Somali
    Democratic Republic. Kenneth R. Redden (ed.) Virginia:
    The Legal System of Africa Series, 1972.

Pestalozza, Luigi. The Somalian Revolution. Translated by
    Peter Glendering. Paris Edition Afrique, 1974.

Potholm, Christian. Somali Politics and Government: Somali
    Nationalism. Cambridge: Harvard University Press,
    1963.

Zartman, I. William. Somali Politics and Government. New
    York: Praeger Publishers, 1963.

JOURNALS

Abbas, S.A. and Djelastik, A.M. "Reports of Food Consumption Survey in Mogadishy City, Somalia." *Fooq.* and Nut'ri tion in Africa. FAO/WHO/OAU, July 12, 1973.

Adua, L. The Civ'il Service in New African States. New York: Frederick A. Praeger, Publishers, 1965.

Alderfes, Harold Freed. Public Administration in Newer Nations. New York: Praeger Publishers, 1967.

Area Handbook presented to the Supreme Revolutionary Council for the Committee on Local Government Reform and Commission on Simplification of Working System of Public Administration in Somalia, 1972 and 1977.

African Contemporary Record of Annual Survey and Documents, African Publishing Co., New York, 1977.

Bennet, Norman R. (ed.) Leadership in East Africa. Boston: University for Africa Research Studies, No.9, 1968. Galied, Ali Khalif.

Bureaucratic Corruption in Developing Countries: A Comparative Analysis and Inquiry. Syracuse, 1972.

Hess, Robert L. "Italian and African Colonial Ambitions in the First World War." Journal of African History IV, 1963.

"Italian Colonialism in Somalia." Located in the Archivio Storico dcll ex Ministerio dell Africa Italiana (ASMAL) in Rome.

Jacomy, mi Uettea. "Is the Institution of Ombudsman Applicable to African Legislation and First Results." Can'a'dian Journal of African Studies. Montreal, 1974.

Kaplan, Irving. "Area Handbook for Somali." June 15, 1969.

Kitterrnaster, H.B. "The Development of the Somali." J'ournal of the African Society 1931-1932.

Lewis, I.M. "The Politics of 1969 Somali Coup." Journill of Modern African Studies. London: XN October 1972.

Lewis, I.M. "The Somali Conquest of the Horn of Africa." Journal of Africa History, 1960.

Lewis, I.M. "Islam in Somaliland: A Pastoral Democracy." London:

Oxford University Press, 1961.

Lewis, I.M. "A Study of Pastoralism and Politics Among the Northern Somali of the Horn of Africa:' From, A Pastoral Democracy. London: Oxford University Press, 1961.

Lungi, Gratian F. and John O. Oni. "Administrative Weakness in Contemporary Africa." Africa Quarterly.

Miller, Norman N. "The Political Survey of Traditional Leadership: Africa Politics and Survey." Basic Issues and Problems of Governmental Development. New York: The Free Press, 1970. Mohamed, Khalief Salad, compiler.

Somalia: A Bibliographical Survey. Connecticut: Greenwood Press, 1977.

Mohamed, Said Barre. "Great Success Has Been Achieved in the Socialist Construction of the Country." New Era Mogadisho, No. 19, November 1974.

Murray, David John (ed.). "Studies in Nigerian Administration." University of ife Nigerian, Hutchinson EducationaL, 1970.

Official Publications of Somaliland 1941-1959. Washington, D.C. U.S. Government Printing Office, 1960.

~ Parkhurst, Estelle Sylvia. "Ex Italian Somaliland." London:
~ Watts Publishers, 1951.

"Somalia Economic Policy," Jobs and Skills Program for Africa, V. XXXXV, 403.

Somali Ministry of Planning and Coordination Development Programs, 1971, 1973. Mogadishu, 1971.

Somali Planning Commission Short Term Development Program, Mogadishu 1969-1970. August, 196B.

"Somali Fights the Shifting Sands." African Development. London, 10 N May, 1976.

"Somali and Arab League." Published by the Ministry of Information and National Guidance, Mogadishu. The State Printing Agency, June 1974.

"Somalia: Economic Development, 1960-1979." Prepared by Dr. Pavle Kenzevic, Project Appraisal Adviser to the State Planning Commission for Project Development and Planning, SOM/7B/00B, Mogadishu, March 10, 19BO.

"Somalia Collected Works," Northeast Africa Series

No.3, September 1953 and March 1975. New York: University Field Staff.

"Somali Democratic Republic." Africa. London, October 26, 1973.

"Somaliland: Italian Administration, Social Political and Economic Aspects." rtalian Affairs, May 1952.

"Somali land Advance under Italian Trusteeship Apprised by United Nations Trusteeship Council." Italy Report on Social and Economic Conditions. Discussion by Advisory Council, July 10, 1952.

Stafford, F.E. "The Ex-Italian Colonies." International Affairs, Vol. XXV, January 1949.

"The Politics of 1969 Somali Coup." Journal of Modern Africa Studies. London, October 30, 1972.

U.S. Department of State, Bureau of Public Affairs, Notes on Somali, N788l. Published by Government Printing Office, Washington, D.C., 1974.

U.S. Information Service. Somali Democratic Republic Country Data, Mogadishu, February 1, 1976.

Walter, Z. Duis. "Africa Administration: Directory of Public Life." Administration and" Justice for the African states, 1978-1979. Published in 3 volumes. New York: K.G. Saur, 1978.

UNITED NATIONS REPORTS

United Nations Visiting Mission to Trust Territories in East
    Africa, 1957. Report on Somaliland under Italian
    Administration. Official records of the 18th and 20th
    Sessions of the Trusteeship Council, New York, 1958.
Report of the Interregional Seminar on the Development of
    Senior Administrators in the Public Service of
    Developing Countries, Vol. 11. (Written for the United
    Nations Conference in Geneva, August 19-29, 1968).
    "African National Development." Report presented by
    Charles M. Thomas to the United Nations in 1967.
Report of Technical Assistance Mission to the Trust Territory of
    Somaliland Under Italian Administration, New York,
    1952.
"Italian Somaliland." United Nations Report on Italian Affairs,
    U.N. Trusteeship Council, 1955.
Syed Naxab Haider Nagvi, "Ethical Foundation of Islamic
    Economic." Isla'llic Studies. (The Journal of the Islamic
    Research Institute, IslamaQad, Pakistan), 1978.
Frithjof Scbuon, Islam and the Perennial Philosophy. London:
    World of Islam. Festival .Publishlng Co , , LTD, 1966.
Seyyed Qutb, "An Islamic Approach to Social Justice." Khurshid
    Ahmed Islam, it's Meaning and Message. London. Islamic
    Council of Europe, 1976.
Muhammad Igbal, The Reconstruction of Religious Thought in
    Islam. Lahore Sheikh Muhammad Ashrof, 1960.
Ibn Khaldun, The Mugaddima (An Introduction to History). Vol.
    11. Translated into English by Franz Rosenthal. London:
    Routledge and Ke~~Paul, 1958.
Nasr, Syed Hossein, Ideals and Realities of Islam. London: Allen
    B. ' Bnwin LTD, 1922.
Mohamed Gamel ElDin El-Fandy, Why I Am a Believer (Cairo,
    Egypt. Ahram ~ss, 1772), 147-157.
AM AI-Qadir As·;;Sufi, the way of Mohamed, Berkeley; Diwat
    Press, 1975, 186.
Moha~d Assad, Islam at the Crossroads (Lahore: Arofat
    Publication, 1964), 7-10.
Seyyed Hassein Nasr, "The Western World and its

Challenges to Islam," in Khurshio Ahmed.,
Islam - Its Meaning and Message (London: Islamic Council of
     Europe, 1975), 217-241.
Abdal-Qadir as-sufi, "The End of a Civilization and After," Islam
     a Quarterly Journal l(hijra l39b) I 3-10.
Syed Hawab Haider Nagvi, "Ethical Foundation of
     Islamic Economies." Islamis Studies~ The Journal of
     Islamic Research Institute, Islamabad, Pakistan, Summer
     1978.
Syed Qutub, "An Islamic Approach to Social Justice." in
     Khurshid Ahmed (sa.) Islam, Its Meaning' and Message.
     London I Islamic Council of Europe, 1976
Muhamed Igbal, The Reconstruction of Religious Thought in
     Islam. Lahore: Sheik Mohamed Ashrof, 1960.
Syed Qutub, "An Islamic Approach to Social Justice," Khurshid
     Ahmed (sa.) Es Lasu Its Meaning and Message, London:
     Islamic Council of Europe, 1976.
Nasr, Syed Hossein, Ideal/3 and Realities of Islam.
     London: Allen & Unwin LTD, 1922.
Caldwell, Lynton K., "Turkish Administration and
     the Policy of Expediency." William J. Siffin (Ed.),
     Toward the Comparative study of Public Administration.
     Indiana University, Departnent of Government.
Chapman, Brian, British Goverriment Obsezved ,
     London: George Allen and Unwin LTD, 1963.
Diaamant, Alfred, "The French Administrative
     System." William J. S1ffin . (Ed.), Toward the
     Comparative Study of Public Administration.
     Indiana University, Department of Government, 1957.
     110ha.ned Algazall, p. 95, p. 102, p. 106. Saudi Arabia.
Islam and Economic Studies by Abu Alaamodudi Lahor,
     1960, p , 11. p. 13, p. 17, p. 62.
Faith and life by Dr. Yausuf Algarthaw1. Published
     1975, Beirut, p. 66, pp. 67, p. 73, pp. 77, p. 93, p.
     164, p .• 166, p. 2.58, p. 203. Brotherhood in Islam by
     Imam AI-Ghazali, 19!ilO. 223
     London Road. By Maurice Bucaille, The Bible - the
     Quran and Science, 1979, p. 22. p. 126. p. 198. p. 231.
Islam Today by Abul Ala l1aud. Daral-~alam. Kuwait,

p. 35. p. 33. p. 36. p. 39. print July 1968.
Othman Araro. deputy parlianent in Kenya. Islamic
League, 1973.
Islam the Religion of Truth by Abdul Rahman Ben Hamad
Alomar, Al Farazdak Press, Riyadth.
The First Written Constitution in the World by Dr.
M. Hamidulla. Muslim Political Thought,
Administration by H.K. Sherwani.
Igbal and the Recent Exposition of Islamic Political
Thought by Dr. Mohaned Aziz Ah~d.
Muslim Contribution to Science and Culture by
Mohaned Abdul Rahman Khan.
t4uslim Colonies in France, Northern Italy and
Switzerland by H.K. Sherwani.
Mohaned Shakir, 1979, publisher Beirut. International-
Review of 11is5ion, VelUllle LXV. No. 260, Oct.
1976. p. 427. 110haned Rasjidi. Ali Mohsin -.
Barwani.
Islamic Movement, Intellectual and Practical Dynamism.
Dr. Mohaned Manzoor Alam.

JOURNAIS, PERIODICAIS AND NEWSPAPERS

Islamic Literature (monthly), Lahore.
Islamic Review (manthly), Woking.
Islamic Studies (quarterly),
Islamabad. Morning News (daily),
Karachi.
Muslim News International (monthly), Karachi
Muslim W or Id (weekly), Karachi.
Q.utb's, 1975. This Religion of Islam. Dar Al
Koran, Beirut.
    100 Khaldun. The Mugaddima. An Introduction to
    History, Vol. 11. Translated into English by
    Franz Rosenthal. London-Routledge and Kegan
    Poul, 19.58.
Nasr, Syed Houssein. Ideals and Realities of
    Islam. London. Allen & Unwin, LTD, 1922.
Mohamed Mohamud Alswaf. Colonalizm and Islamic
Struggle. Published Muslim League in Meca, 19650
The Straight Path. Hussein Abbara. Published 1978.
Mohamed Algazali. Published Cairo, 1966, p. 2), p.
    147, p. 199.
Maududis, A.A. Toward Understanding Islam.
Nadwis, A.A., 1973. Islam and the Word.
Islamic Economic Theories Practiced by M.A •.
    Mannan, June 1970.
Hakim Khalifa A. Islam and Communism, Lahore,
    1962.
Ibn Khaldun, al Mugaddlima; 5th chapter.
Smith, W.C. Islam in Modern History, Princeton
    University Press, 1957.
Ahmed Mohamed Jamal. Lecture about, Islamic Culture,
    p. 205, p. 28), p. 297.
    Published King Abdulaziz University.
Islamic Movement in Africa by Dr. Hasan ISA
    Abdathir. Published 1981, Saudi Arabia.
A1masonia by Ahmed Abdi, Aikafur Atah, Islamic
    League, Published 1.978.
Dr. Hanunudah Abdalti, p. 126, p. 1)0. The World

Assembly of MtiSlim Youth, Riyadth, Saudi
Arabia, 1960. .

Contributo alla Konoscenza delia Preistoria della Somalia e dell
"Ogaden "Atti delia Societa Toscana di Scienza Natural!."
Voll. XLVII. Pisa 1938-39, 133 p. Blanc, A.C.
and'Tavangi, G. Brown, C. and Burkitt, MC Stone
Implements from British Somaliland "Man." Vol. XXXI.
London, 1931, 156-9 pp. Coniglia, G. Note Storiche Sulla
Ci tta d , Mogadishu "Ri vista Coloniale." Roma, 1917.

Cerull, E. Di alcune nwnete raccolte sulla costa Somala. "Rivista
deglistudi Orientali," Boma, 1924, 281-2 pp.
Iscrizioni edocu",nti arabi per la storria della Somalia.
"Rivista deglistudi Oriental1." Vol. XI, Roma, 1~26, 1-24
pp.

Nuovi documenti arabia per la storia della Somalia. "Rendiconto
Reale Accademia del 11nce1." Vol. II, Ser No. 0, Roma ,
1927, 392-410 pp. La Littadina di Mercca e tre sue
Iscrizioni arabia. "Oriente Moderno." Anno XXIII. 20-28
pp. La Somalia Hallana nell antichita classica. Palermo,
1910, Casparo, A.

Die Goldlander Punt und Sasu im Somaliland Das Ausland. Vol.
XXVII-XXIX. 521-528-660 pp.

Governo della Somalic Maseo della Garesa: Catalogo. Regia
Stamperia della Colonia Mogadischa MCMXXXI-XIII,
177 pp Ills maps. The Somali Conquest on the Horn of
Africa. "Journal of African History." No.2, London, 1960,
213-230 pp. Mathew, G. The Grcheological Situation in
East Africa (Somalia), "Antiguity." Gloucester, 1953.
Nella Vecchla Brava. "Somalia d'oggi." N. 3. Mogadishu,
1957, p, 12. Mohamed, Vama (Ha~hi). An introduction to
Somali History from 50GO years R.G'. down to the
present time, Mogadishu, 1961, p. 62. Appunti di Storia
dell, "Africa" (Somalia) Anno di Studi, 1960-61. Insti tuto

Universistorio della Somalia Facolta di Magistero. Edizioni "Bi
erche," Boma, 158 pp bibl. Touval, S. Somali Nationalis:
international politics and the d:i:'ive for 'uni-ty,~in the
Horn of Africa. Harvard Uni versi ty Press,
Cambridge, 1963. "~po. 214.

Lewis, I.M. The names of God in northern Somaliland. Bulletin

of the school of Oriental and Africa studies. Vol. XXII,
    Part 1, University of London, 1959, p.,139~140.

Ferrand, G. Les Comalis' Matriaux d 'Estudes
    s'ur les pays Musulmans leroux, Paris. 1903.

Note sul movimento Muslmano in Somalia. Rivista degli studi
    Orientalia, Vol. X. Fasc No.1, Roma, 1923. p. 1.
    Cerulli, E.

Banca d'Italia La Banca d'Italia nelle Terre
    Italiane d'Oltreroare, Somalia, page 89.103,
    Roma, 1940, S9-103. grophsills.

Camera, Di, Commercio, Agricolutla ed industria
    Della Somalia. 11 Credito Somalo nel, 1955.
    Bolleltino Mensile Camera di Commercio' N 4-5
    Mogadishu, 1956.

Cassa per la circolazione Monetaria delia
    Somalia. 1 Espercizio Sociale. 18 Apri le,
    1950. 31 Dicember, 1951. Istituto
    Poligrafica dello stato. Rama, 1952, p. 134.

Somali Commercial Bank.Bulletin (special issue). Tipo Lito
    Missione Mogadishu. Oct.1971.

Somali Development Bank. Final Report of Richard G. Leonard r
    Adviser. 1966, 1970. Mogadishu.

Cerull, E. Testi di diritto consue tudinario dei
    Somali Merrehan. "Rivista degli Studi Orientali." Pasco
    N. **4.** Rama, 1918.

Ciamarra, G. Justice indigene dans la Somalie Italienne.
    "Bullettetin de Calnisation Comparee." Bruxelles, 1912,
    385-400 pp.

Bertola, A. Confessionismo religioso dir, iti umani nella
    Costituzione Somala. "La Comunita internazionale," Vol.
    XVI, Roma, Luglio, 1961.

Leggi Fondamentali Per 'La Somalia Assemblea legislativa della
    Somalia, Mogadishu. 1956.

Mohamed Scek'Cabiou La nostra Co~tituzione Stamperia
    Missione. Mogadishu Giug No. 1961. Brown, A.J.
    Adoption of Islamic in Somaliland Protectorate, Hergisa.
    1956.

Corte Di Giustizia Della Somalia. Norme per Qadi Stanperia del
    Eoverno Mogadishu. 1957.

Mohamed Noor H. The rule of law in the Somali Republic. "Journal of the International Commission of Jurists." Vol. N. 2, Eeneva. 1964. p. 276-302.

Abdirizak, Hagi Hussen, La questione dei confine dopo sei anm , "Somalia d':o£;gi." No. -7, Mogadishu, 1956, p , 14.

Administrazione Feduciaria Italiana Della Somalia Testo della Converzione Fiduciaria Peril Territorio della Somalia sotto Administrazione Italiana AFIS, Roma, Marzo, 1950, p. 61.

Industrial Production Ministry of Planning and Coordination, Central Statistical Department, r·logadishu, 1974, p • .58.

Handcrafts of Somali, Editors Abdilsalam, H. Adam and Rugia Siad. Ministry of Industry Publication. Tipo-Lito Mission, Mog~uUsht\t 1972, p. 22.

Mohamed Jama (Habasrn.) Economic Survey of Samali, Hogadishu, 1970" N. 4, p. 8S.

Somali Democractic Republic, Our Revolutionary Education: Its strategy and objectives. State Printing Agency, 1logadishu, June 1974. Foreign Trade Year 1976, Central Statistical Department, Mogadishu. Manpower Survey Project. (4 vols.) Ministry of Labour and Sports. Labour Department, Mogadishu, August 1972.

Pachal B. The International Aspects of South African Indian Question, Captow: Struik, 1971. 318 pp.

Pillay, B. BritiSh Indians in the Transvaal: Trade, Politics and Imperial RelatiOns, 1885-1906. Longmans, 1976, 259 pp. Deklerk, 11 .A. The Puritans in Africa: A History of Afrkanerdom. Hormondsworth: Penguin in Association with Rex Collings, 1975. 376 pp.

Kapungu, L.T. United Nations Ecanomic Sanctions as an Instrument of Peace Enforcement: With Special Reference to Rhodesia. University of London (External), 1972.

Comaroff. J:L. Competition for office and political process as among the Barolong Boo Ratshidi of South African-Botswana Borderland, University of London , 1973.

Che-Mponda, Aleck Humphery. The Malawi-Tanzania Border

and Territorial Dispute, 1968, a case study of boundary and territorial hyperactive in the New Africa. Howard University, Washington, D.C., 1972.

Joffe, Selby Hickey. Political Culture and Communication in Malawil The nortatory regime of Kamuzu Banda, Boston University, Mass., 1973, pp. 6)2.

Schram, E. Volkenrechtliche Aspekte des Rhode sipnron fliktes. University af Munich, Fed. of Germany, 1970.

Ogene, Francis Chidozie. Group interests and United States foreign policy on African issues. University of Cleveland, OhiO, 1974, p. 403, 95, 538, 1337, 1992, 1993.

Coger, Dalvanmoe. The international politics of Apartheid South Africa at the United Nations, University of South Carolina, Columbia, 1970, p. 196.

Africa by Jamal ~I. Ahmed Africa by Abiikadir Hamza Bofe Islamic Government by Dr. Zatlir Ryadth Inside America by Dr. Saleh AbU Alfatah, publisher Dar Al Hanar. 1986. Jedah, Saudi Arabia, pp. 136. pp. 136. pp. 139. pp. 161. pp. 169. pp. 177, pp. 183, pp. 183, pp. 185. pp. 193. pp. 198. othman Dan Fodiuo

Mohamed Dan Fadiuo published in Sudan Fulani. Translated in Arabid, Islamic Studies Library Abdulla Biaro (Kanu) Nigeria Islam Studies (Kanu) Mohamed Juneid (Sokoto)

al-Ittihad, Volume 18, July-September 1981 - Mohama Tarig Quraishi. 2 Islamie Revolution of Iran: Personalities and Coneepts. Ibid., pp. 32-33 of Artie1e. The Russian Fight for the "luslim Soul, All-Itthad. Volume 18, NUIlber 2.
Mohamed Assad, Islam at the Crossroads, Lahorer Arofat Publication, 1964, 7-10. Seyyed Hassein Nasr. "The Western World and its Challenge to Islu," in Khurshid Ahmed., Islu its Meaning and Mes6~e (London: Islamie Council of Europe, 1975), 217-241. Ablal-Qad1r As SuFi, "The End of a
Civilization and After." Islam. a Quarterly Journal 1 (Nijira 139b): 3-10. Ibid., pp. 3-10.

MANUALS, REPORTS AND" PAPERS(Prepared by the Somali Institute of Public Administration (SIPA) at the request of the President of the Somali Democratic Republic} entitled, "Promotion of Research, Exchange of Information and Other Activities Necessary to Accelerate Improvements in Administration and Development."

1) An Index of Somali Legislation from 1967-72.
2) Manual on "Methods of Improving Efficiency" •
3) Manual on "Duties and Responsibilities of Personnel Officers Working *in Ministries* and Agencies" ;
4) Manual 'On "Registry and *Filing"* •
5) "Role and Responsibilities of Top Executives in the Political, *Social* & Economic Development of Somalia." Final reports prepared at workshops held at the orientation course for top executives.
6) List and Functions of *Public* Agencies *in* Somalia.
7) Brochure on the Objectives and Activities of SIPA.
8) Brochure of Administrative Changes in Somalia (1971-72).
9) Annotated Bibliography in Public Administration.
10) A glossary of Administrative Concepts and Terms *in Somali* Language.
11) Trade Promotion.

MANUALS, REPORTS AND" PAPERS(Prepared by the Somali
Institute of Public Administration (SIPA) at the request of
the President of the Somali Democratic Republic} entitled,
"Promotion of Research, Exchange of Information and Other
Activities Necessary to Accelerate Improvements in
Administration and Development."

1) An Index of Somali Legislation from 1967-72.
2) Manual on "Methods of Improving Efficiency" •
3) Manual on "Duties and Responsibilities of
Personnel Officers Working *in Ministries* and Agencies"
4) Manual 'On "Registry and Filing*"*
5) "Role and Responsibilities of Top Executives in the Political,
Social & Economic Development of Somalia." Final reports
prepared at workshops held at the orientation course for top
executives.
6) List and Functions of *Public* Agencies *in* Somalia.
7) Brochure on the Objectives and Activities of SIPA.
8) Brochure of Administrative Changes in Somalia (1971-72).
9) Annotated Bibliography in Public Administration.
10) A glossary of Administrative Concepts and Terms *in Somali*
Language.
11) Trade Promotion.

Made in the USA
Middletown, DE
24 March 2016